TO LOVE AND TO HONOR

B. J. HOFF

LIFEJOURNEY
BOOKS

Acknowledgements

My thanks to the Library of the United States Military Academy,
West Point; particularly to Mrs. Marie T. Capps, Map and
Manuscript Librarian, and to Kenneth W. Rapp, Assistant Archivist.

LifeJourney Books™ is an imprint of Chariot Family Publishing,
a div. of David C. Cook Publishing Co.
David C. Cook Publishing Co., Elgin, Illinois 60120
David C. Cook Publishing Co., Weston, Ontario
Nova Distribution Ltd., Newton Abbot, England

TO LOVE AND TO HONOR
©1986, 1993 by B.J. Hoff

Cover design by Turnbaugh & Associates
Interior design by Glass House Graphics
Editing by Penelope Stokes

First Revised Printing, 1993
Printed in the United States of America
96 95 94   5 4 3 2

Library of Congress Catalog Card Number 86-071122
ISBN 0-78140-406-1

For Jim
A man of honor beyond words

Seek those rare and priceless gifts
only heaven can impart—
Love and Honor—God bestows
these timeless treasures of the heart . . .

B.J. Hoff

CHAPTER ONE

Kerry O'Neill tugged in vain at the long skirt of her faded plaid cotton dress, wrapping her black cape more closely about her as another in a series of shivers ricocheted down her spine. The sharp October wind blowing in off the water stung her face. Longing to see the end of this reluctant journey, she wondered if the steamboat would soon be nearing West Point.

Trying to ignore the churning of her stomach, she bit nervously at her lower lip and read once more the letter which had reached her in Buffalo only a few weeks after the death of her da.

. . . and so I am enclosing what I trust will be sufficient funds to see you safely to West Point, Kerry. My housekeeper, Molly Larkin, and I are extremely pleased that you will be making your home with us. . . .

So it would not be Mr. Andrew Dalton assuming guardianship of her, but his son, Mr. Jess. Or should she be calling him "Reverend," since he was the chaplain of the United States Military Academy?

With an uneasy sigh, she transferred her attention from the letter to the breathtaking, untamed beauty of the Hudson Highlands around her. The sweeping wind and low-hanging clouds made the huge rocky cliffs on either side of the river seem even more forbidding. Sure, and this strange river had none of the sweet peacefulness of Lough Leane in her own County Kerry. No, this Hudson was an unbridled, wild thing with a purpose of its own, gouging and winding through a savage, intimidating land. Again she shuddered, no fault this time of the cold afternoon.

She tugged at the hood of her cape, attempting to ward off as much of the wind as possible. At the same time, she returned her attention to the letter. The chaplain *did* sound kind, she thought, not too terribly staunch and military as she feared he might be.

. . . I know all this must seem very strange to you, finding yourself in the care of a man you've never met; but the friendship between your father and mine was special, and both of them were anxious to provide you with more than a token of security. . . .

Indeed, it had been a special, if somewhat unusual, friendship, Kerry mused, tucking a copper curl back to its hiding place beneath the hood of her cape. Conor O'Neill, her Da, had saved the wealthy lawyer's life during a brawl on the waterfront when Mr. Andrew was engaged in one of his many crusades to assist the dock workers. From that day on, he and Conor had been good friends and comrades in the young labor movement rising up all across the country. Mr. Andrew's home was in New York City, but he visited them in Buffalo when he was there on business; he and Conor wrote to each other frequently.

While the friendship had been a source of enrichment and satisfaction for both men, it had become a thorn in

Kerry's side. It was responsible for her being in this embarrassing and frustrating situation, one which would continue until she reached the age of twenty-one.

. . . Therefore, the guardianship agreement was prepared in such a way that in the event of his death, my father's next of kin would take responsibility for you until you come of age. I am his only son, and he made me aware of this agreement some months before he passed away. I want to assure you that I am more than willing to provide for you the home and security my father would have given you had he lived. You will be most welcome to stay with us, Kerry; we eagerly await your arrival. . . .

A guardian, indeed! And she a grown woman of eighteen. Oh, certainly this Mr. Jess sounded nice enough. He had mentioned in the letter that Molly Larkin, his housekeeper, was from Ireland; that would be a comfort, surely. But what a predicament, to be depending upon a strange man who undoubtedly had enough of his own problems.

Her Da, of course, intended it only for her good, arranging with Mr. Andrew to care for her if anything should happen to Conor before she was grown. But now that the possibility had become a reality, she fervently wished she could find a way out of it. Having to impose upon Mr. Andrew would have been bad enough—although at least she had made his acquaintance and was comfortable in his presence. But now, with him passed on, it was positively degrading to be carted off to his son, a man she'd never seen—and him a man of God, at that.

She folded the letter into a small rectangle and stuffed it up the long, closely fitted sleeve of her dress, glancing warily about her once more. As the steamer finally left the wilderness, passing around the point which gave the Academy its name, Kerry looked longingly behind her just once more, as though to say farewell to her past life.

No more would she hear her da sing songs of the misty,

green countryside of Ireland when they were both feeling a bit homesick. Never again would he play his flute and make that soft, sweet sound like the evening wind dipping down across the gently rolling hillsides of their farm. No, that was over now, and she would—she must—lay it to rest and go on.

With a determined lift of her chin, she raised her eyes to a plateau above the west bank of the river, gaping in amazement as she beheld the spartan stone buildings of the United States Military Academy. Had it not been framed by such breathtaking beauty—massive old rock cliffs, enormous, towering trees waving their crimson, gold, and bronze colors like the flags of many nations, and a brilliant azure sky with sharply drawn clouds—it would have been depressingly austere.

Kerry slowly expelled the breath she'd been holding and straightened her shoulders. *This is what da wanted for me,* she reluctantly admitted to herself, *so I'll be making the best of it for his sake. But I'm thinking it would be a mite easier were the place less gloomy to look upon. . . .*

The gangway was drawn up almost as soon as she and two other travelers stepped onto the dock. Kerry looked anxiously about her surroundings. She supposed the Reverend Mr. Dalton would be easily recognized—a man of the cloth, he'd most likely be a graying, dignified sort.

Her eyes darted here and there, but she saw no one fitting such a description—only a tousle-haired giant leaning against a somewhat dilapidated wagon, his lips pursed in an idle whistle, his hands thrust into his pockets. Kerry appraised the colossus with a twinge of distaste. A dockworker, she decided. He looked none too friendly, with his curly, windblown mane of black hair, thick dark beard, and broad, massive shoulders hunched forward against the wind. Certainly he was no gentleman, standing indolently in his shirt-sleeves and work trousers as though it were the middle of summer.

When the big man suddenly straightened and started toward her, she looked anxiously around for the army officer or the young man who had been aboard the steamer with her. But they were already making their way up the path, and no one else was nearby. Whatever would she do if this mountain of a man were one of those louts who preyed upon young girls alone? Where *was* that Reverend Dalton, anyway?

As the man approached, she met his gaze for an instant and was startled by the astonishing depth of feeling she encountered in his eyes. Flustered, she looked quickly away, unnerved by the odd mixture of kindness and power, sadness and peace, that looked out at her.

Certainly he doesn't intend to speak to me, she thought. *He would not dare to be so bold.* But now he stood no more than a few inches away, scrutinizing her. Kerry stared resolutely at her feet, refusing to acknowledge his presence, desperately wishing for someone—anyone—to appear and rescue her.

"Kerry? Kerry O'Neill?" His voice was rich and soft with a smoothness that belied his powerful appearance.

How could he know her name? Who was this disreputable-looking man with his odd, gentle voice? Forcing herself to look up, she eyed him suspiciously. "I'm Kerry O'Neill." She thrust her chin firmly upward. "And who might be wanting to know?"

An unexpected smile brightened the giant's face. With a touch of surprise, Kerry saw that his eyes—incredibly, brilliantly blue—appeared to hold a wealth of gentleness.

"I'm Jess Dalton, your guardian, Kerry. Welcome to West Point."

His large hand, easily twice the size of her own, reached out to hers, but she was too bewildered to accept it. *It could not be,* her spinning mind protested. *This towering, plainly dressed workman could not be a chaplain—certainly*

9

*not the chaplain of the United States Military Academy—
and the fine gentleman who was now her guardian!*

The broad forehead below the incorrigible black hair furrowed with concern. "Are you all right, dear? You've gone white as a sheet!"

Dear! As though she were six years old. She fought to regain herself. "I—I'm fine, sir. Yes, I'm fine. I—It's just that I wasn't expecting someone like you . . . ." Blast! Now she'd been rude. He'd think her a country mouse for sure!

His wide, firmly molded mouth turned up in amusement. "Exactly what kind of person were you expecting, Kerry?"

There! She was right. He would be having himself a bit of fun with her. Well, they'd see about that, they would.

Her eyes snapped as she mustered all the dignity available to her. "A gentleman of the cloth was what I'd been led to believe, sir." She glanced pointedly at his tan, slightly rumpled work shirt which strained across his broad shoulders.

He gave her a rueful grin. "Ah . . . I don't quite resemble a proper chaplain, do I? I'm sorry about my appearance; I was puttering about the house, fixing a few things, and didn't have time to change. I should have, I know." Then, as though he could read her thoughts, he added, "But I am Jess Dalton, Kerry. Entirely trustworthy, I assure you."

The look she fastened on him was one of disparaging doubt, but she held her tongue. He had called her by name and had mentioned the guardianship, so he must be the chaplain. Indeed, he wasn't at all what she'd expected, but the fact remained that she was in the man's custody for a time, so it would be best not to cause any more resentment on his part than was absolutely necessary.

"Where's the rest of your luggage? I'll put it in the wagon, and have one of the cadets bring it up to the house later."

"This is my luggage, sir; this is all of it," she replied,

indicating the worn, frayed valise she'd carried off the steamer. "There's a trunk of my da's things, but I couldn't arrange to bring it just yet. My neighbor in Buffalo, Mrs. Glendon, is keeping it for me for the time being."

"I see. Well, then, I'll just carry this with us," he answered, tucking the valise under one arm. "It's not a bad walk from here, so long as you don't mind the dust."

He smiled kindly, taking her arm to guide her up the path toward the Academy. "My housekeeper, Molly, is most anxious to see you. She's spoken of nothing else but your coming ever since you wrote."

He went on making friendly conversation in his soft, rich voice while they walked. "Kerry, I was so sorry to hear about your father."

"Thank you, sir. And I was saddened to learn about Mr. Andrew, too. He was such a fine man. I understand he was ill for many months."

Jess nodded. "Yes, he was. He struggled quite a long time before his body finally gave up." He shook his head briefly before continuing.

"It was difficult, watching him waste away as he did. He'd always been such an active man—too active at times. I think there was more agony for him in the confinement than in the physical pain."

He glanced down at her with a smile. "They were great friends, weren't they—your father and mine? I often felt as though I knew both of you. He talked so often of you and your father. He admired Conor O'Neill greatly, you know."

"Mr. Andrew was a wonderful man, sir. He visited us when he was in Buffalo, and having him at the flat was always a grand treat. He never failed to bring a few fascinating stories and a great deal of laughter with him."

Jess smiled wistfully at her words. "Yes, the Lord blessed him with a generous sense of humor."

They walked on in silence, except for his soft whistling.

Kerry attempted to study him discreetly as she hurried to keep up with his brisk, long-legged stride. What a tall fellow he was—at least four or five inches over six feet. She found his unconventional appearance rather intriguing. His unruly dark hair with its random streaks of silver at the temples looked as though it would be difficult to tame. She would have expected him to be clean-shaven and more dignified looking. Still, she could see he carried a firm, square jaw beneath his neatly trimmed beard. His nose had an arrogant thrust which made him appear a bit stern. But his eyes were captivating. All in all, she found him an impressive, interesting man, though somewhat formidable.

"Kerry, I want you to know you're most welcome here. Molly is especially happy you'll be living with us; she gets lonely, you see. There's a dearth of women at West Point."

She flushed guiltily, hoping he hadn't noticed how she'd been staring at him. "Oh, thank you, sir. I do appreciate what you're doing for me. It's just that I'm sorry Da felt he had to impose upon you like this."

She wished with all her heart that she could be independent and not a burden. But things were not always the way she would order them. At least for now, she must try to be agreeable and cooperative. Later she would look about for employment. In a place like this, there must be a way for a strong Irish colleen to support herself.

As if he had read her thoughts, the chaplain said, "I wouldn't want you to ever think this is an imposition, Kerry." He broke his stride and turned to look down at her. "Your home is here now and I want you to be happy with us. Besides, you'll be good for Molly and me, I'm sure of it."

"You're being very kind, sir, and I'm grateful for your generosity." His words were comforting, but she couldn't bring herself to look into those expressive eyes. Instead, she stared down at the tips of her worn black shoes until he touched her arm to urge her forward.

"Another thing: please don't call me *sir*. It makes me feel like a drillmaster. I hear enough of that from the cadets. They're required to use the term, but you're not. After all, we're practically family now. My name is Jess, and that's what you're to call me."

"Aye, sir—Jess. Thank you."

"Just ahead is what we call the Plain." He gestured toward a large, dusty field. "It's the main parade ground."

There was very little to mark it as anything special. It was simply a flat piece of ground, barren of trees, with only nondescript stone barracks flanking it. But quite a variety of activity seemed to be going on in the area. At one end, staccato drumbeats echoed in a precise cadence while uniformed cadets called marching orders to young men in gray. Smaller groups of men drilled separately at the other end of the field.

Kerry almost jumped out of her shoes when a nearby cannon exploded. Jess laughed and caught her gently by the arm. "You'll get used to all the noise in a few days, Kerry. If nothing else, it's orderly noise."

Overhead, the sky unexpectedly darkened to the same gray as the uniforms of the men, draping the Plain and its surroundings with a strangely dark, oppressive appearance. An unbidden shudder coursed through Kerry as it occurred to her that this stark, alien place, so lacking in any touch of softness to relieve the grim harshness of its atmosphere, was now her home.

No. She rebelled at the idea. She could not yet bring herself to apply so warm and comfortable a word as *home* to this cold rock of a place.

But the uneasy chill lifted when she again focused her attention on the cadets drilling on the field. She was impressed by their smart formations, their ramrod postures, and their synchronized movements.

Jess smiled at her obvious fascination. "Tonight, if you like, we'll walk over from the house and watch the evening parade. I think you'd enjoy it."

"Oh, yes, I'd like that, I'm sure! My, there are so many of them. And see how fine they march, so straight and even. Why even their noses are lined up in proper rows!"

Her enthusiasm charmed him. She was refreshingly young and candid, though far from being the child he had expected. His father had often referred to her as a "delightful child," and he had come to think of her in that way. But there was nothing childish about her appearance. True, she was petite and pert and delicate. However, she was nothing less than lovely, an observation which caused a flicker of concern to nag at him.

That thick auburn hair pouring out from the hood of her cape and those dancing green eyes were going to turn many a young man's head, he feared. And she had such incredibly beautiful skin.

He suddenly felt awkward with her and irritated with himself. *I've been alone too long,* he thought, then almost laughed aloud at his own foolishness. Hardly alone—with a corps of cadets and wonderful, motherly Molly. Still, the girl was like a welcome breath of spring. Definitely refreshing. Definitely delightful.

He stole another glance at the small, intriguing creature hurrying along beside him. The he set his gaze straight ahead, deliberately ignoring the almost overwhelming protective instinct which those narrow shoulders and small, dainty hands seemed to call forth from him. He was suddenly anxious to deliver her into Molly's responsible care, ridiculously eager to begin their new life together as a family. A strange mixture of anticipation and contentment settled over him, and he walked even faster.

14

CHAPTER TWO

They entered an iron gate and approached a porch that ran the length of a large, cream-colored stucco house with long, brown-shuttered windows. At the same time, a tall buxom woman with thick braids of silver on top of her head came bustling through the front door to meet them, her sensible, gray skirt swooshing behind her.

When she called out to them, her sharp voice was thick with Irish brogue. "Well, then, and are you finally coming? 'Tis giving up on you, I was." Her tone was stern, but Kerry saw with relief a faint twinkle in her dark eyes.

"Hush, Molly, you'll frighten our girl away before she even gets inside the house," Jess reprimanded with a grin. "Kerry, meet Molly Larkin, who is about to take you under the very sturdy shelter of her wing."

With ample arms, Molly gathered Kerry into a firm embrace, unfastened her cape as she talked and paid no heed whatever to her employer. "Ah, lass, and you're naught but a whisper in the wind, you're that thin," she clucked solicitously. "Come in now, let's be getting you some food and drink. You must be fair to drop after your trip up the river." She pulled Kerry along through the door and into the hallway, leaving Jess to follow behind.

They entered a large, cheerful kitchen where an enormous pine table was set for the midday meal. Molly took the valise from Jess and tucked it into a corner.

"Take the lass to the pump now, Jess, so that the two of you can freshen yourselves before you eat," she ordered brusquely, pushing Kerry toward the chaplain. She hurried over to the wood range to check a boiling pot. "Sure, and the pork is more than done by now."

Jess winked at Kerry and led her to a small, bricked pantry off the kitchen, whispering close to her ear. "She may come across as a terror, but she's an absolute lamb if she takes a fancy to you. Since she decided to adopt you long before you ever arrived, you've nothing to worry about except that she'll mother you to distraction!"

Kerry smiled and splashed some water onto her hands. "She'll be a comfort, I'm sure. It's been some time since I've had anyone fuss over me."

"What of your mother, Kerry?" he asked kindly, handing her a towel. "I don't believe I ever heard my father speak of her."

"I'd not be remembering my mother, I fear. She died when I was still a babe. I do not even know what she looked like, but my Da used to say I had the fresh-air skin of her British raising."

"Your mother was British? That doesn't happen often, does it—a marriage between the two?"

The slight husky catch in her voice he found so charming was even more pronounced when she answered him. "Theirs was a real romance, some say. Conor O'Neill stole his own landlord's youngest daughter—at least he stole her

16

heart. They ran away to County Kerry to be married. Her family disowned her, of course, but they were that much in love it didn't matter to them."

"And you were born there?" His direct blue gaze reflected genuine interest in her story.

"Aye, I was—on the farm where we lived until we left our country to come here. I was named for the mountains, y'know." She glanced out the small, narrow window of the pantry before continuing.

"It hardly seems possible that we've been gone for three years. 'Twas in the summer of 1839 when we first set foot upon American soil. So much has happened since then."

"Were there no other children?"

Her bright green eyes clouded for a moment. "My older brother, Liam, began the voyage with Da and me, but he was always frail, and the journey was too much for him."

He touched her shoulder lightly. "I've heard about the conditions on the ships coming from Ireland. Was it very bad for you, Kerry?"

When she turned her gaze to him, the flood of bitterness in her voice and the naked pain in her eyes stabbed like a knife through his chest.

"Bad? Oh, aye, it was bad, all right! 'Twas the only time in my life I've been treated less kindly than an animal, I can tell you."

"What do you mean? What did they do to you?"

"We were packed onto the ship like so many cattle—no, no, they'd have been more considerate of cattle. We'd no fresh air, never enough clean water, only spoiled food most days. And there was so much illness, such disease. . . ."

Her voice, tight with anger, drifted off, and she turned slightly away from him. "Because we were so poor, you see. We could not afford proper traveling accommodations."

Gently, he turned her around to him. "And your brother? He died at sea?"

17

She stood stiffly, looking down at her hands while still clutching a small towel. "Aye, he did. The weak ones—like Liam—had no chance." Raising her eyes once more to his, a spark of anger flared. "No chance at all! They made us beg, you know. They made us beg just for rotten food—so we could stay alive. And some of them would laugh when they saw us grieving for our dead."

She supposed that since he now knew the full extent of her family's poverty, he would look down his nose at her just as so many others in the city had. *Well, let him, then.* After three years, she had become almost indifferent to the sly whispers and insinuating laughter she often encountered on those few occasions when she ventured out of her own neighborhood in Buffalo.

Her da had rebuked her often enough when she complained to him about their circumstances. "'Tis no sin in bein' poor, darlin'. The sin is in bein' ashamed of it. Don't y'ever forget, Kerry Shannon—no matter how poor we are, we're clean, we're honest, and we fear God. We need no more reason to be holdin' our heads high with the rest of the decent people in this new land. Let no one bow your head, girl. No one."

In spite of her da's frequent reassurances, she found it incomprehensible that people—nice people from fine backgrounds—would take such an immediate dislike to her and others like her simply because she was from another country. She wanted so much to be a—a good citizen, a proper American. Sure, and it would be taking some effort on her part, but didn't her da say she was a bright girl and could learn anything she put her mind to? All she needed was a bit of time.

She swallowed hard when it occurred to her that her new guardian might well be one of the very ones who found immigrants so disreputable. Hadn't Da told her many

18

times about the wealth and fine reputations of the Dalton family? But would a chaplain, a man of God, be thinking in such a way? She peered up at him defiantly, wondering for a moment what feelings the bottomless depths of those mysterious eyes held.

Lost in his own thoughts, he had turned away from her. He had heard a variety of stories about the immigrants and their crossings, and he was aware of all the tales which hinted of the vile, even inhumane treatment they received on board ship. A number of times in New York City, he'd seen for himself examples of blatant prejudice toward the "foreigners" coming in ever-increasing numbers to the shores of America. He knew the Irish, in particular, had been singled out as targets of some of the most vicious resentment ever unleashed upon an ethnic group. They were blamed for everything imaginable simply because they were "different"—and usually poor.

But his always empathetic, sensitive nature stirred with a new depth of indignant anger at hearing firsthand the confirmation of all he'd been told, bringing the ugliness of prejudice to his own front door. This slight, guileless girl with her direct gaze deserved better. He intended to see to it that from now on she would be protected from such cruelty.

Frowning at his back, Kerry feared that she'd been right, that he now found her presence distasteful after learning about her less-than-proper background. The expression in his deep-set eyes was unfathomable when he turned to face her once more, and Kerry wished he would say something to prove her wrong. Instead, he took her arm and led her back to the kitchen, deepening her feeling of regret.

However, her disillusionment was temporary once she got a good look at the table heaped with salt-cured pork and cabbage, boiled potatoes, and warm applesauce. Two freshly baked fruit pies sat cooling on the shelf of a large white cupboard, their rich aromas combining with those of the dinner to make her mouth water in a most unladylike fashion.

"Ah, now, lass, you and Jess be getting some of this food into you! There'll be time enough later for talk. Eat now while the steam is still on it," Molly commanded. She pushed Kerry into a chair while motioning sternly to Jess to take his usual place at the head of the table.

Once she'd recovered from the shock of seeing Molly sit down at the table as though she were a member of the family rather than a housekeeper, even offering an "Amen" to Jess's prayer of thanks, Kerry wasted no time in filling her plate. She ate as though she were starving; indeed, she nearly was. For weeks, she had been forced to watch every cent with extreme care. She had almost exhausted the last of her da's pocket money.

Molly observed the girl carefully, nodding her approval once or twice, then pushing another helping at her. Kerry was so involved in the delightful taste of Irish cooking that she very nearly forgot her disappointment with Jess. Nor did she notice how sparingly he ate.

Molly, however, didn't miss his unusual indifference to her cooking or the intense way he was studying the young woman across the table from him. The housekeeper's keen eyes narrowed with interest when she saw a spark in Jess's gaze—a spark she hadn't seen for years.

"And what is it with your appetite, my Jess? Have you suddenly been taken with a fever?" she asked pointedly.

Caught off guard, he looked up at her with a sheepish grin. "How can I eat a hearty meal when you insist upon plying me with this Gaelic grub?"

Kerry looked at him with surprise; her words tumbled

out before she thought about them. "You're not Irish, then, sir—I mean, Jess?"

"Me? Irish?" He smiled vaguely at her. "Why would you think that?"

Kerry colored. Something about the man, she decided, defied what she knew of his impressive family background, his extensive education and influence. In spite of the refinement that so clearly marked his manner, there was an unexpected earthiness to the man sitting across from her. It was more than his size, more than his obvious virility or the aura of physical strength he wore so easily.

"No reason, I'm sure," she muttered hastily, pretending a great absorption in her second helping of potatoes.

"Humph!" Molly snorted. "Don't be listening to him now, lass. He may have been born on this soil, but his blood reaches back into Eire as far as one can search it out, it does. And he's usually eating twice what he ought when I cook a good Irish dish. He just seems preoccupied today for some unknown reason."

A firm knock at the kitchen door halted Jess's retort. As Molly rose from her place at the table to open the door, Kerry's eyes widened with interest at the handsome young cadet who entered and stood at attention before Jess. With undisguised curiosity, she studied his black cap and gray uniform with its black herringbone trim and gilt buttons. He had a fine face, she thought, in spite of his ramrod posture and the peculiar way his chin was doubled.

"Mr. Dalton, *sir*—" His voice was stiffly formal, but he focused his dark brown eyes warmly on Kerry, who glanced down at her plate for a moment before returning her gaze to him.

"Sir, the Superintendent invites you and your guest to view the evening parade with him later. He would appreciate the pleasure of being introduced to your ward, sir."

Molly interrupted. "Her name is Kerry O'Neill, Mr.

Teague. *Miss* O'Neill to you, young man. Now, why don't you just unpuff your chin a bit and have some apple pie with us before you return to duty?"

The cadet glanced hopefully at Jess, who smiled and nodded his approval. "Sit down with us, Mr. Teague, and enjoy your pie."

Kerry watched, fascinated, as the young man's face quickly changed from the stiff, military bearing of a cadet into a boyish, good-natured grin. "Thank you, sir. I'll have to hurry, though. You know I'm not supposed to eat any-where but in the mess."

"Humph! And rightly named it is, with the abominable stuff they force on your poor lads." Molly sniffed indignant-ly as she cut a huge piece of pie and thrust it at him.

The cadet cleared his throat before taking a bite of the pie. He looked pointedly at Kerry, then at Jess, who wiped his mouth slowly, hiding a smile behind his dinner napkin.

Finally, he offered an introduction in an amused tone. "Kerry, allow me to present Cadet Teague—Edmund Teague, from Philadelphia. Mr. Teague is a member of the illustrious senior class."

Kerry looked into the young man's friendly dark eyes for a moment, then lowered her gaze. Mrs. Glendon, her elder-ly next-door neighbor in Buffalo, had taken it upon herself to give Kerry some sorely neglected instruction in the art of being a lady. One of the lessons she had impressed upon her was the need for a young woman to avoid meeting the eyes of a gentleman for any length of time, although she had never explained why.

Studying the cadet's clean-shaven face, which seemed all angles and smooth planes, she decided he was a fine man to look upon. Most of all, though, she liked his mischie-vous smile and the twinkle in his eyes. He seemed to hold some delicious secret tucked away just waiting to be shared. Something told her that this lad wouldn't be one to

22

think of her as any less than what she was.

"I'm very pleased to meet you, Miss O'Neill. I hope you'll be happy here at the Academy," he said between hurried bites of pie. "Molly, this is wonderful. I'd starve if it weren't for your handouts, I swear I would. It's a positive sin what they expect us to eat. Uh, sorry, Mr. Dalton, sir."

Turning quickly back to Kerry, he declared enthusiastically, "Miss O'Neill, I'd be greatly honored to show you around the Point when I have some free time, if you'd like."

Jess's smile faded. "Thank you, Mr. Teague, but I'll see to it that Kerry—Miss O'Neill—learns her way around the grounds," he said firmly.

Why, he sounds positively stuffy, Kerry thought with surprised irritation. Looking directly at the cadet, she stated emphatically, "Thank you all the same, Mr. Teague. Perhaps I'll be seeing you here from time to time."

Glancing at Jess, she saw a somewhat startled look cross his brow. *Oh my, I've been forward, I suppose. But still, he was a bit heavy-handed with this nice young man.*

After the cadet had gone, Jess cleared his throat awkwardly. "Kerry, you'll have to understand that you won't be able to have anything to do with the cadets except perhaps at an occasional social function. The rules here are quite strict—rigid, actually—and the young men are allowed no leeway." He rubbed his big hands together and looked down at his plate as he continued.

"You'll be a source of . . . great interest to the men, of course. They don't see many pretty girls around here. You'll need to be on your guard about that, I'm afraid."

Was he saying he thought her pretty? The thought was intriguing. Da had never actually told her whether she was or wasn't. As close as he'd ever come to an opinion on her looks had been once, when she was no more than fourteen or so, and she had asked him straight out.

His reply, half of forever in coming, wasn't what she had hoped to hear. "Well, now, I suppose you're a fair enough lass, Kerry Shannon. But it'll serve ye well to be remembering that looks is good for but a brief time, but a pure heart is good forever."

"Rubbish, Jess!" Molly's sharp voice shattered Kerry's reflection. "Don't be makin' the lads sound so disreputable." She bustled around the table, clearing off dishes with efficient swoops of her strong arms.

"Pay him no mind, lass. It's his job to tend to the proper behavior of his men. He does it well enough most of the time, though he can be as feisty as the lot of them. It would seem he's takin' his position a bit more seriously today, for whatever the reason." She ignored Jess, who glared at her for a moment, then rose from his chair.

"Kerry, if you like, I'll show you to your room. I expect you might want to rest before evening." His gaze was inscrutable as he held her chair and waited for her to rise and follow him.

He led her up a sweeping staircase with massive, intricately carved balusters, rubbed to a satin sheen, and then to a small, lovely room at the end of the hallway.

"Oh, it's so grand!" she exclaimed with delight. "I've never seen such a fine room. I'll not be wanting to step foot out of it."

Her eyes grew wide with wonder as she took in each detail: the rose and gold-leaf wall covering, the white marble mantel with its gracefully curved opening around the fireplace, and the bright-colored rag rugs scattered throughout the room. A fire had been laid in the fireplace, and the overall effect was one of cheerful comfort and feminine grace.

Clasping her small hands together under her chin, she paced quickly about the room, fingering a few pieces of furniture with a gentle, almost reverent touch. She turned

24

to Jess with dancing eyes that couldn't begin to hide her pleasure.

He smiled warmly, pleased with her excitement. "Molly's been a busy bee for days now. She has a way of getting the best out of most things, houses or people." His tone of voice left little doubt about his admiration for his housekeeper.

"You rest now, Kerry—as long as you like. We'll be doing some walking later this evening if you feel up to it." He lightly cupped her shoulder with his big hand when he walked by her, and she felt a surprising skip to her heart when she saw the tenderness in his eyes.

"Kerry—I'm truly glad you're here," he began somewhat hesitantly. "I'd always hoped for brothers or sisters, but it wasn't my good fortune to be blessed with them. I'd be honored if you'd look upon me as your brother. I promise I'll do whatever I can to make you happy."

After Jess had gone, Kerry sat down on one side of the bed, shaking her head slowly, looking with awe around her new bedroom. Why, she'd never had a room of her own in her entire life! On the farm, she'd had a mere corner of the kitchen behind a blanket Da had hung for her privacy. And in the flat where they lived in Buffalo, she slept on the sofa, leaving their one bed for Da, a big man who needed the room to sleep comfortably.

Her mind reeled with the strange new situation in which she found herself and the unfamiliar feelings coursing through her. It seemed true enough that the Lord had placed her in the care of kind and generous folks. She felt as though she'd known Molly all her life. And Jess—well, he couldn't be much nicer, although he seemed a bit strange. He appeared to like her well enough; yet she felt he was keeping some distance between them. Perhaps that was why he made her feel . . . uneasy.

Fatigue readily overcame the anxiety she felt about her

25

strange new situation and the excitement of the day. She removed her shoes, then sank gratefully onto the plump, comfortable bed.

I don't much like being obligated to others, Lord, or having to depend upon anyone but Da or myself . . . but if this is to be the way of it for a while, I thank You that the two of them are so kind. . . .

Soon, she drifted off the sleep, to dream of her da's cheerful smile, a steamboat, and gentle, sad blue eyes that seemed to look into her heart.

Sandwiched between Jess and the Superintendent, a pudgy little man with a rather large nose and nervous mannerisms, Kerry's eyes sparkled with excitement as she watched the memorable spectacle of the sunset parade.

For a few moments, she forgot about being homesick or missing her da, caught up in the rich history and tradition marching in front of her. Her small foot kept time with the precise beat of the cadet band, and she thrilled at the sight of so many proudly uniformed young men, their cap plumes catching the blaze of the slowly descending sun, while bayonets and muskets flashed metallic reflections all across the field.

Why, it's like a parade of wonderful toy soldiers, she mused, smiling at her own fanciful thought. *Aren't they fine, all spit and polish, like perfectly carved little men?* She marveled at the way even the leanest of cadets sported a minimum of two chins, sometimes three, with their shoulders back and their heads pushed into their chests as they marched. *What a grand sight,* she decided, thrilled by the deep male voices as they barked commands while the drumrolls echoed across the Plain and one of the most spectacular sunsets she'd ever witnessed bathed the entire scene in a glorious array of colors.

Beautiful, her heart whispered reverently. *So beautiful . . .*

not at all the grim place it looked to be earlier today. . . .

At her side, Jess quietly watched as he had so many times before. But this evening his face was set in an expression of deep brooding, his eyes clouded with the mist of something he attempted to shake off.

The bronze and golden shimmer of the lowering sun seemed to stop, suspended about the field of marching men in front of him, as though to paint them upon an entirely different canvas in another scene, in another time . . . . And suddenly the rosy hue transposed to a violent, brutal crimson. The splendid, thrilling portrait before his eyes became a heart-chilling nightmare, a battlefield where a bloodbath was occurring . . . . The very cadets who had paraded in proud, precise formation now lay suffering and dying in some dreadful, sinful war . . . . Fathers murdered their sons, and entire families lifted their hands against their neighbors. A man wept over his brother's body, slain by his own hand . . . .

He heard the tormented cries of the soldiers' agony; he felt the chilling touch of hands grown cold. He walked among the silent bodies of young men—mere boys—who had once marched together and sung stirring songs together and saluted a flag now torn asunder, a flag that had become two flags, as a pitiful remnant of survivors lifted wooden steps and marched to a mournful cadence that echoed doom. . . .

"Jess? Are you all right?"

His heart might have ceased to beat, he thought, had not the small, warm hand tugged at his elbow. Kerry's soft, worried voice dispelled the fiendish vision from his mind.

He made himself pat her hand and smile weakly. "Yes, of course, dear. I'm afraid I have a tendency to—daydream at times." *What have I seen, Lord? What have I seen if not the very vision of my most hideous fears for this country?*

An icy hand enveloped his heart and squeezed. *What kind of war, Lord, . . . what kind of war would it be when friends kill friends and brothers slay brothers upon the very fields where they once played and worked together?*

The sight of her freshly scrubbed, beaming face was the salvation of his sanity. His blood seemed to thaw and commence its normal flow through his body as he allowed himself to drink in the innocent light in her eyes. Her small, pursed mouth and her fine-boned form gave a misleading impression of fragility. But he suspected that strength was woven throughout every fiber of her being.

Finally, after what seemed an outrageously long time, he smiled, noticing how the fading light of the evening sun cascaded over her hair, turning the tumble of copper waves into a fiery aura about her.

At that moment Jess suddenly realized, with great surprise, that he had been lonely—perhaps for a long time. He realized it only because it occurred to him that, since the arrival of Kerry O'Neill, he no longer felt the loneliness that had subtly draped itself around his heart many years ago.

CHAPTER THREE

It was difficult for Kerry to realize she'd known Molly Larkin no more than two weeks. Helping to tidy the kitchen after Sunday dinner, a veritable feast, she chattered and asked questions as though Molly had been a part of her life forever.

Her questions centered almost entirely around Jess. After attending the worship service in the chapel with Molly earlier that morning, Kerry's mind had been filled to overflowing with thoughts of her new guardian.

She had been somewhat disturbed by the man in the pulpit as she watched him and listened to his fervent, impassioned sermon. He hardly seemed the same person as the cheerful, kind-natured man she'd come to know about the house. At home he was informal and soft-spoken, given to unpretentious work clothing and relaxed manners. He had taken to ruffling her hair in a teasing, affectionate way or tugging her by the hand when he noticed something he thought she'd enjoy during their walks around the Point. He had indeed assumed the role of an older brother in her life, cautious of her feelings and protective of her welfare.

Although she was still bewildered by the way her heart seemed to race in a most peculiar way at the slightest attention from him, she was nevertheless growing more and more at ease with him as time passed. In truth, her hours with Jess were by now her favorite times of the day.

But in the pulpit that morning, he had appeared so tall and commanding as he raised a hand to explain a point or lifted his Bible in a way that seemed to dare any one of the young men in the chapel to ignore its truth. Watching him, Kerry had experienced a strangely anxious, oppressive sensation—much like the feeling that had gripped her when she first looked upon the imposing chapel.

Right away, she had felt dwarfed and somewhat threatened by the size and dignity of the imposing gray structure with its enormous pillars. Once inside, she had been even more overwhelmed, hearing the cadet choir of male voices raised in perfect harmony as the strains of "O God, Our Help in Ages Past" echoed between the stately Grecian columns. A sense of wonder and awe invaded her entire being. She looked raptly around the impressive interior, taking in everything from the finely carved altar rail to the black marble tablets containing the list of West Point graduates who had honorably served their country in times of war. She whispered furtively to Molly, asking about the one name which had obviously been removed.

"'Tis where a traitor's name was once displayed," Molly explained as quietly as her voice would allow. "Benedict Arnold was his name; he betrayed his country—our country. And so he lost his place of honor here in this chapel, as indeed he should have."

But when Jess finally began to offer his sermon, Kerry was even more astonished. Gazing up at him, her mouth slightly agape, she thought her heart would surely stop when she saw how his eyes flashed with the fervor of his words. But even greater was her surprise when she became aware that he was saying things in his sermon that might be directly related to her experience on the ship coming over.

Listening intently, hanging onto his every word, she realized moment by moment that what she had interpreted as disgust that day in the kitchen when he'd questioned her about her voyage might actually have been an emotion more akin to anger. Leaning forward on the hard, wooden seat, the one position that allowed her feet to touch the floor, she barely moved except to occasionally stroke the soft green wool of her one good skirt or to squeeze her hands together with excitement.

". . . If you take nothing from the pages of God's Word"—here he raised his black leather Bible high for emphasis—"except this one vital truth, it alone will ennoble you and perhaps enable you to live a decent, worthwhile life. That truth is this: In the eyes of our Creator, we are equal." That one word echoed like a chant. *What a glorious word,* Kerry thought. *"We . . . are . . . equal."*

Jess's eyes burned into the gaze of every person in the chapel, one by one, as his words grew more and more heated. "I believe with all my heart that ignorance breeds prejudice . . . and prejudice breeds inhumanity . . . and inhumanity eventually breeds war! Today, in our cities, in our villages, even on the frontier of our country, an ugly, destructive disease runs rampant. That disease is prejudice—and it will destroy the very fiber of America's freedom if we do not somehow halt its spread.

"We are turning on the very ones who look to us for refuge. We continue to scorn and despise the immigrant who comes seeking freedom from poverty. We have done *nothing* to correct the deplorable, shameful conditions

31

these brave people endure just to make their way to us. And then, if they're fortunate enough to survive their journey to our country, we meet them with the dehumanizing blow of bigotry!"

His words continued to hammer away like physical blows. "Do you know—have you heard what some of these brave people go through merely to survive? And look . . . God forgive us . . . just look and see what we are doing to those whose skin is a different color from our own!" He shook his mane of hair in a gesture of great sadness. "They plead for freedom from their misery, dignity for their families, and instead, America—a country conceived by the very concept of God-given freedom and rocked in the cradle of liberty—continues to enslave the bodies and the souls of those created by the same One we call Father."

He leaned forward, far over the pulpit. For a moment the strong, noble features of his face were overshadowed by a stark, agonized image of grief. "We are fools if we believe we can escape the consequences of our inhumanity, our ignorant cruelty."

Kerry was so caught up in his message, in the excitement of hearing such power unleashed and poured forth over a subject so dear to her heart, that she very nearly missed one of the most significant facts—at least to her—of his entire sermon. When it finally hit her like an unexpected, surging wave, she could have jumped from her seat with a spurt of great relief and joy.

On the first day of her arrival at the Academy, when she had described to Jess her voyage from Ireland, the strange anger she had sensed in him had not in any way been directed toward her and the undesirable facts of her background. No—Jess had simply been moved and troubled, not because he found her poverty offensive, but because of what he had only a few minutes before referred to as inhumanity.

Oh, and hadn't she misjudged him terribly? What a great relief it was—this once—to be so wrong. Sure, and wasn't he a fine, honorable man—a wonderful man . . . to care so much?

As she and Molly discussed the morning, Kerry questioned a term the older woman had used to describe Jess. "What d'you mean, that he's a new breed?"

"Well, now," Molly replied, deftly balancing several plates on her arm while she stepped quickly across the kitchen to the massive white corner cupboard, "I've been told that most of the chaplains before our Jess were nothing if not proper and dignified—and a few somewhat boring! Sure, and you saw this day that our Jess is something of a firebrand in the pulpit. He feels his faith strongly, he does, and can't share it in a milksoppy fashion. Besides," she declared with obvious pride, "he's head and shoulders above any of the others in his relationship with our Lord. Some men only talk about what they believe—but our Jess lives it, he does. That's why he's always spending so much of his time writing his papers and books—"

"He writes books?" Kerry questioned, her expression revealing the fact that she was immensely impressed by this new discovery.

"That he does, lass." Molly's own admiration for her employer was reflected in her proud, dark eyes as she lifted her chin. "You should be knowing that our Jess is a famous man, known for his stand against the owning of slaves and the terrible abuses against innocent children and women in the factories—even if it does get him into a bit of trouble from time to time."

Kerry stopped sudsing the crock in her hands. "What kind of trouble?"

Molly shook her head and lowered her voice. "There are those, lass, who don't want to be hearing certain of our

33

Lord's commands, only those they find comfortable and easy to live with. Our Jess is known all about the East and even beyond for his writings and his power in the pulpit. But that doesn't necessarily make him a popular man, if you'd be understanding what I mean."

"You mean some people don't like him because he wants to help those folks who are being mistreated?" Kerry asked incredulously.

Molly stopped putting the dishes away for a moment, flicked an imaginary bit of lint from her dark brown dress, and looked at Kerry. "'Tis a shame to have to admit such a thing about this country, lass, but the truth is that an honorable man like Jess Dalton is no hero in certain places. Of course, that makes no difference to him—he'll fight to the death for what he believes. But it's a worry, all the same. Sometimes I fear for him ever finding any peace, especially with him being so alone and still grieving over his poor Miss Emily . . . ." She shook her head in sadness as she continued to stack the remaining plates in the cupboard.

Kerry felt an odd twinge of apprehension. "Who's Miss Emily?"

"She would have been his bride had it not been for the terrible accident. And her such a perfect mate for him, too."

"What happened to her?" Kerry asked, slowly drying her hands, then tucking her white muslin blouse more firmly into the waistband of her skirt.

Molly clucked her tongue and replied, "Mind that you don't go mentioning it around him, now. His grief is still like a sharp-edged knife, even though it's been five years and more since she were taken." Removing her apron, she took it to the door and stepped outside to shake out any crumbs. Returning to the kitchen, she continued her story.

"'Twas a fall while she was riding the fine young mare her daddo had given her. She and our Jess often rode together, you see, them being fond of the horses. Ah, you never saw a sadder sight than the poor lad when they told him about the girl. I had been working for him and Mr. Andrew but a few years when it happened, but I knew him well enough already to see that it fair destroyed him."

"He loved her greatly, did he?"

"Oh aye! They had grown up together, their families being good friends. To my knowing, he has never cared for another but his Miss Emily, God rest her soul. Sometimes it's near impossible, understanding the way of things like that."

Kerry moved to the window, looking out upon the bright, crisp autumn afternoon. Why did it seem to pierce her heart, hearing that Jess had once loved someone so much? Perhaps it was because she was beginning to care for him deeply—as a brother, of course.

"Was she—a pretty lady, his Miss Emily?" Kerry asked softly, keeping her back turned to Molly.

"Pretty, indeed—beautiful, she was." Molly continued to bustle around the kitchen, replacing the soiled dinner cloth with a clean one, then straightening the chairs around the table. "And such a lady. Why, she played many a musical instrument, and she read the same important books that our Jess reads. Her family was wealthy too, as was his, and so she'd been raised in a fine, proper way."

How very awkward and unpolished I must seem to him!
Kerry swallowed with difficulty, puzzled by why it should hurt so much to think of Jess's looking upon her in such a disparaging way. *How he must miss her, if he loved her as Molly says,* she mused sympathetically. *That must be why his eyes are so terribly sad. . . .*

She heard his soft, rambling whistle as he came through the kitchen door, stamping his feet on the mat before Molly had a chance to chastise him for "dragging the outdoors inside."

35

"Well, now that you ladies have everything cleaned up, I believe I'm ready for some of that custard pie." His voice held a light, teasing note that invited a retort from Molly, who didn't disappoint him.

"Sure, and I might have guessed it! It never fails but the minute I finally get to sit and catch my breath, in he comes needing something or other."

Jess, his eyes twinkling merrily, shared a grin with Kerry as he unbuttoned the collar of his white shirt and tossed his black suit coat onto a nearby chair. "Ah, now, Molly, I merely want a small piece of pie. But if it's a problem, I'll wait until later—" He shrugged and uttered an exaggerated sigh, lifting his brows at Kerry in a signal that they both knew what was coming.

"Indeed you will not!" Molly declared firmly. "I'd not be hearing the end of it before midweek if I were to deprive you of your Sunday sweet, I'm sure. Well, go on, then. Sit down and I'll fix your plate—*again.*"

Jess pulled a chair back from the table, giving Kerry's shoulder a light pat before sitting down. "And what have you been up to, little one?"

"No—nothing," she muttered, vexed by the awkward stammer his affectionate touch had brought on.

Still, she was pleased when he gestured to the chair beside him. "Here, sit down. I'll share my pie—you need it far more than I do."

He speared a bite of pie with his fork and placed it against her lips, grinning as she obediently popped open her mouth to accept the tasty morsel.

She sat watching him eat, enjoying the way he seemed to relish each bite. "More?" he questioned.

When she shook her head, he smiled and finished off the pie. "Minding your waistline, are you?"

"What d'you mean?"

He wiped a crumb from her mouth with his napkin.

"Nothing, dear. I'm just teasing you."

Kerry felt a familiar, frustrating pang of rejection, just as she always did when she failed to understand him right away. If only she were educated and smart, as Molly said his Miss Emily had been. Clenching her hands tightly together in her lap, she stared down at the table.

"Well, I'm going to walk off this pie now. Want to come, Kerry?" Not waiting for an answer, he caught her hand as he stood up and pulled her to her feet.

"Get your cape, dear—that sunshine is misleading. The wind has picked up considerably this afternoon."

As they started down the winding path behind the house, he noticed her slight shiver and draped his arm casually about her shoulders in a brotherly fashion. "Beautiful, isn't it?" he asked, glancing around contentedly.

Like a soft breeze, gladness washed over Kerry at his unexpected, affectionate touch. "Aye, it is. And you love it here, don't you, Jess?" Her eyes were bright with fondness as she looked up at him.

"Why, yes. Yes, I do," he agreed, smiling at her. "I was once a cadet, too, Kerry—did you know that?"

"You? A cadet?" she exclaimed with astonishment. "But you—you're a chaplain!"

He nodded, his smile widening. "But I haven't always been a chaplain, Kerry. My father wanted me to have the education offered by the Academy—not to mention the discipline." He lifted his dark brows in a self-mocking expression. "I'm afraid I was somewhat of a rebel in my younger years, you see."

He laughed when he saw her shocked look of disbelief. "Oh yes, it's true."

"But if you were learning to be a soldier, what made you decide to become a chaplain?"

His gaze moved slowly away from her to the rugged

cliffs beyond them. "Somehow I knew that I was meant to fight in a different way, not as a soldier. Even while I was studying military strategy and drilling for hours with the other cadets, I sensed the Lord calling me to a different kind of life."

Returning his attention to her, he smiled at her serious, intent expression. "And what about you, dear? Do you like it here by now?"

Two weeks had made a difference. The endearment that had once irritated her now gave her unwarranted pleasure. "Oh, of course I do," she said quickly. "You and Molly have been wonderful to me."

He searched her eyes for a long moment. "But you're not all that happy with us yet. Are you?"

"It isn't that," she said with a sudden rush of confusion. "I'm not . . . unhappy, Jess." It was true. She had come to care a great deal for him and for Molly. Their combined efforts to make her feel welcome and at ease with them had quickly warmed her heart with a measure of well-being. How, though, could she make him understand— when she wasn't sure she understood it herself—that she nevertheless felt humiliated by the dependency that had been forced upon her?

"Kerry?" he probed gently, the understanding smile in his eyes inviting her confidence.

Her breath caught in her throat when he raised a work-calloused hand to graze her cheek lightly with a surprisingly tender touch.

"I—I do like it here, Jess. Truly, I do. It's just that . . ."

He moved then to enfold both her small hands between his much larger ones. "It's just that you miss your father, don't you, dear?"

"Aye, I do," she admitted with a small sigh. "He was my whole life, you see, for so long. . . ."

He gently squeezed her hands, implying that he understood. "No one expects you to forget him or stop missing him, Kerry. But I do wish you could get over your resentment of my guardianship."

Caught off guard at his perception, she pulled away from him, her eyes sparking with defiance. "You do not understand, Jess—you cannot." The words tumbled from her before she could stop them. "You've most likely never had to depend on anyone for anything. I never thought I would, either. From the time I was but a wee thing, Da drilled it into me to stand with my head high and take care of myself. Why, he was forever making a fuss about self-respect and independence. But look what he went and did to me! Tell me how I can be taking care of myself when I have to lean on you or Molly for every small thing!"

He longed to draw her close to him, to soothe her frustration and erase the hurt in her eyes. Instead, he spoke softly, but firmly. "Kerry—you must accept what your father tried to do for you, the provision he made for you. His intentions were the best, don't you see? He was only trying to protect you, to provide you with a future."

"I understand that," she admitted grudgingly. "But he shamed me, nevertheless."

Unable to meet his eyes, she glanced down at the ground, only to feel his index finger gently lift her chin, raising her face to his. His voice, customarily so rich and confident, was strangely hoarse and uncertain. "Kerry, don't ever say that. Don't you know how much you've come to mean to . . . to Molly and me? How much we want you with us? Why, your father gave us a gift—"

For one fleeting instant the force of his gaze seemed to draw her next to his heart. But the sweetness of the moment was suddenly shattered. A tall, good-looking cadet strode briskly up to Jess, addressing him at attention, while at the same time darting a look of contemptuous interest at Kerry.

CHAPTER FOUR

"M r. Dalton, *sir*—"

"What is it, Martin?" Jess asked irritably.

"I'm sorry to . . . interrupt, sir . . . but there's been a fight between one of the plebes and Cadet Sergeant Burns. Sergeant Burns is badly hurt, sir, and is asking for you." Once his message was delivered, the cadet boldly turned his disturbing hazel eyes away from Jess to examine Kerry.

Kerry's gaze was drawn to the classic planes of his lean face. *He's an elegant-looking man,* she thought. *But what is it about him, fine-looking as he is, that makes me feel as chilled as a winter day in the mountains?* She decided it was his eyes. His eyes were incredibly cold.

"Kerry—" Jess's voice broke into her assessment of the cadet. "I'll have to go right away. You'd best return to the house now."

"If you like, sir, I'll be glad to escort the young lady back to your house," Cadet Martin offered politely.

Kerry saw Jess hesitate an instant before answering. Glancing quickly at her, his gaze then darted about their surroundings. "Perhaps you should. We've walked out farther than I'd thought to. Kerry, you go with Mr. Martin, and I'll attend to Mike Burns.

"Where is he?" he asked the cadet.

"In front of the stables, sir. Two upperclassmen are with him."

As Jess hurried away, Martin turned to Kerry and courteously offered his arm, which Kerry instinctively ignored. "Miss O'Neill?" he prompted.

Something about his manner made Kerry uncomfortable. She found herself avoiding his touch and glancing surreptitiously up at him out of the corner of her eye every few steps.

"How do you like it here by now, Miss—O'Neill, isn't it?" he asked smoothly.

She could feel his eyes on her, and an uneasy look at him revealed a cold disdain which made her catch her breath with surprise. "It's a fine place," she replied cautiously.

"Tell me," he inquired in a tone that sounded, Kerry thought, less curious than insinuating, "are you and the chaplain related?"

Darting a suspicious glance at him, she answered, "No, no, we're not. He's my guardian."

"Ah, yes . . . your guardian."

Kerry decided at that exact moment she did not like Cadet Martin at all. Not at all. There was something . . . tainted about the man. Deliberately, without breaking her stride, she moved a few inches away from him.

"How nice for Mr. Dalton—to have the . . . comfort of your companionship. It's a difficult life for a chaplain, I'm sure, being alone so much."

The subtle change in his voice made Kerry glance uneasily about her surroundings, wishing for a familiar landmark; she had no idea how far they might be from the house. She grew even more anxious when they entered a thickly shaded pathway. The foliage of enormous, overhanging trees darkened the place, and thick, gray clouds had moved in to hide the earlier sunshine. Not another person was in sight. No sound broke the eerie stillness except the rapid pounding of Kerry's heart, which she was certain the cadet could hear. She longed at that moment to be at home with Molly, snug and warm in the cheery contentment of the kitchen.

"Is it a different way you're taking me, Mr. Martin? I don't recall being here before."

He flashed white, even teeth in a caricature of a smile. "Just a brief departure. I thought we'd make our way to Flirtation Walk." In spite of her quick step away from him, he grasped her arm firmly and continued walking.

"Jess said I was to return to the house right away, Mr. Martin. I think I'd best do that, if you don't mind," she replied as firmly as possible, determined to give him no hint of the fear that had begun to wash over her.

Maintaining his rapid pace, the cadet continued to grip her arm. "And naturally you never fail to do whatever Mr. Dalton tells you."

"I'll be thanking you to direct me home at once, sir." Annoyed, she tried to pull away from him, but she proved no match for his superior strength. He simply tugged her that much closer to his side.

"Haven't you ever heard of Flirtation Walk, Kerry? You don't mind if I call you Kerry, do you?" he asked mildly, without so much as a glance in her direction.

Glaring furiously at him, she snapped, "No, I have never heard of your whatever Walk—and, yes, I *do* mind. I mind very much, as a matter of fact! Now let go of my arm and take me to the house at once—I *insist!*"

He chuckled lightly, ignoring her demands. "Cadets like to take their sweethearts to Flirtation Walk. It's a very special place—very romantic. Most young ladies think it's a distinct honor to be taken there." Abruptly, he halted on the path and pulled her roughly to him, yanking off his cap as he lowered his face to hers.

Shock surged through Kerry, only to be swiftly replaced by rage. She slapped Martin's face with all the force she could muster, then stepped back and turned to run. But he grabbed her, clamping his fingers down so tightly around her upper arm she shrieked with pain.

He swore as he locked her against him in an ugly embrace. "Now, now, don't get your Irish up, little colleen. I just want to get to know you better, that's all. In fact, I'd like to know you very well, indeed. Come on, now, drop the act—there's no one around to impress."

With arrogant confidence, he made another attempt to kiss her, but this time she defended herself ruthlessly by kicking him in the shins with all her strength. Caught off guard by the force behind her blow, the cadet lurched toward her, his face purple with rage. "You little Irish baggage! No more games, now—"

Just as he would have forced his unwanted kisses on her again, a large, sullen-looking man appeared behind him and jerked the cadet's arms roughly enough to dislocate them, pinning them behind his shoulders. With wide-eyed relief, Kerry watched the steely-eyed stranger in the gray uniform of the plebe hold her attacker firmly from behind, lashing out at the cadet in a hard, threatening voice.

"You'll not touch her again—*sir!*" he shouted, his words edged with scorn. "What is it with you, anyway—does it make you feel more a man, frightening young girls?"

Yanking Martin's arms even more tightly behind him, the plebe looked at Kerry with concern. "Are you all right, Miss?" Kerry nodded uncertainly as she rubbed the arm which ached from Martin's rough grasp.

Her defender released his hold on Cadet Martin and pushed him roughly away. "Unless you'd like those arms broken, *sir,* I suggest you get out of here—*now!*"

"You crazy plebe! Do you realize what you'll get for attacking an upperclassman? You're as good as dismissed right now. Haven't you learned anything in the few months you've been here?"

When the cold disgust in the plebe's eyes didn't waver, Martin lowered his voice somewhat and offered appeasingly, "It's not as though she's a lady, you know. She's just the chaplain's little Irish. . . ."

The other man clamped a massive iron fist over the upperclassman's arm. "Perhaps you ought to be thinking about what will happen to you when Mr. Dalton finds out who attacked his ward. It just may not be the Board who deals with you, *Mister.*"

The significance of the words seemed finally to penetrate Martin's anger. Slowly he backed off, then turned and stamped angrily away under the plebe's cold, level stare.

Kerry's rescuer turned to her and gave her an old-fashioned, gentlemanly bow. "Tom Jackson, Miss. May I help you home now?"

Gratefully accepting the arm he offered, Kerry fervently hoped her weak, shaking legs wouldn't fail her until she was safely inside the house.

Molly was waiting at the door when they walked onto the porch. She pounced upon them, exclaiming, "Where in the eternal creation have you been, lass? And whatever is going on? I've had three cadets here in just the last few minutes, raving about a fight and a man about to die and Jess making arrangements to have someone moved down river. And you nowhere in sight!"

Spying Tom Jackson for the first time, she turned her fury on him. "And just what is this, Mister? What are you doing here?"

Kerry tried to calm her. "It's all right, Molly. Mr. Jackson brought me home because—"

"Miss O'Neill has had a fright, ma'am." Tom interrupted, hearing Kerry's faltering voice. "With your permission, I'll stay and explain to the chaplain exactly what happened. But for now, I think she could do with something hot to drink."

Molly looked him over carefully before taking a firm grasp on Kerry's arm and motioning the plebe inside. "Well, don't just be standing there looking at me, then! Let's get in and take care of the girl. Jess will be spitting fire, he will, when he sees the look about her. Inside, inside!" She fairly pushed him through the door, drawing Kerry more gently along beside her.

The three of them were sitting around the kitchen table when Jess came in, out of breath from hurrying in the cold.

"Molly, I need—"

He stopped as he noticed their peculiar expressions. Glancing from one to the other, he asked hesitantly, "Molly? Jackson? What are you doing here?" He rubbed his hand over his beard, waiting for someone to answer him.

Tom Jackson rose from his chair right away. "Mr. Dalton, sir, there's been a—a problem with Cadet Martin." His face was solemn and disapproving.

Jess waited for an explanation, looking first to Jackson, then to Kerry. Clearing his throat, Tom began again. "Sir, I happened to come along when—"

Kerry broke in, irritated with Jackson's slow, methodical speech, yet sympathetic with the difficulty he was having in finding words to express the situation. Her face flamed with embarrassment and anger as the words tumbled out.

"Mr. Martin took it upon himself to give me a tour of the grounds—a place called Flirtation Walk, I believe. He . . . well . . . Mr. Jackson came along just in time, you see—"

"In time for what?" Jess's usual good-natured expression underwent a remarkable change. His jaw locked in a rigid vise, and he ground out his words in a hoarse, clipped tone. "What happened?"

Molly's anger and indignation exploded. "If it had not been for Mr. Jackson here, our Lord only knows what might have happened! You must *do* something about this, Jess."

Kerry saw Jess clench and unclench both his big fists as he turned to her, fury darkening his eyes. "Kerry, I told you you couldn't have anything to do with these cadets."

She cried out sharply, horrified by the accusation and anger in his words. "'Twas you who sent me with him! I could have come back to the house on my own, you know. But, no—you have to treat me like a child. You told me to go with him, Jess, you—" She broke off, pushing her fist against her mouth, too hurt to continue.

The anger that had clouded his eyes faded. He stood staring down at her as though he were appalled at his own words. "I'm sorry, Kerry. You're right, of course; I wasn't thinking. It's just the shock of coming home and hearing all this." When he would have reached out with a reassuring touch, she flinched and pulled away. Rueful understanding settled over him. "Kerry . . . are you all right?"

"I'm perfectly fine," she choked out, wishing the lot of them would simply leave her alone. She had been with them only two short weeks and just see the trouble she'd caused.

Jess turned reluctantly to Tom Jackson. "Tom—come with me, please. As soon as I give some instructions to the men taking care of Sergeant Burns, we'll need to see the Superintendent about Cadet Martin. Molly, I think Kerry should lie down." He cast an appealing glance at his house-keeper, who nodded in agreement.

"Come along, lass; let's get you upstairs for a rest. You

47

must forget all this now. 'Tis all done. Jess will take care of everything."

Kerry followed along dutifully, her head throbbing. *They both treat me like a wee wane. I'm nothing but a burden to him—to both of them. Oh, I do hate this, being no more than a—a weight about Jess's neck!*

Numbly she continued up the stairs to her room, where she collapsed onto the bed, saying nothing as Molly tucked her beneath the quilt and smoothed the copper tendrils of her long hair away from her forehead.

"Try to sleep a bit, lass. We don't want to worry our Jess, do we?" Molly crooned gently.

Kerry turned her head away so Molly couldn't see the hot tears scalding her cheeks. *No, we mustn't worry our Jess,* she agreed silently, with a bitter taste in her mouth.

CHAPTER FIVE

After helping Molly with the supper dishes, Kerry ventured into Jess's study looking for something to take her mind off the incident with Lowell Martin. The chocolate-brown draperies were closed against the gloom of an early dusk, and she lit the fat beeswax candle on the large, mahogany fall-front desk. Hesitantly moving about the room, she lightly touched a few things, enjoying the sense of being alone in Jess's favorite room, surrounded by those items of which he seemed most fond.

Her fingers glided over the Massachusetts shelf clock on the mantel, lingering on the painted glass panel. She then went back to the desk to examine a brass paperweight, a letter opener with a carved handle in the shape of a saber, and a small wooden figure of a lamb.

This was the first time she'd done more than merely peek into the room, although Jess had told her to help herself to any of the books she found interesting. She picked up the worn Bible lying open on his desk, curious to see what he'd been reading. Glancing down at the page, she scanned the second chapter of James until she came to the verses he'd underlined: "If ye fulfil the royal law according to the scripture, *Thou shalt love thy neighbour as thyself,* ye do well; But if ye have respect of persons, ye commit sin. . ."

Then her gaze fell upon an edge of white lace protruding from the back of the Bible. She pulled gently on the material, discovering a lady's delicately embroidered handkerchief wrapped around a few dried rose petals. *This was Emily's, of course,* she thought sadly. She carefully replaced it, her heart aching for the sorrow he must have experienced.

Browsing through the books on the shelves behind his desk, she was intimidated by so many volumes. Most of them were large and appeared to be scholarly tomes of great difficulty. *'Tis like a university in here, I'm thinking. All these important books—so many. And Jess has probably read them all.*

But Molly had said he also wrote books. With renewed interest, she began to search the shelves for something with his name on it. Discovering a thin volume which looked to be newly bound, she took it off the shelf and opened it to the title page: *The Common Shame of Slavery by Reverend Jess A. Dalton, Chaplain,* USMA.

Kerry hugged the book to her and plopped down on the floor, placing the candle from the desk beside her. She tucked her long skirt around her legs, pulled her black shawl closely about her shoulders, and began to read, halting at one of his statements to try and grasp its full meaning: *The abhorrent practice of slavery destroys both the owned and the owner. It crushes the spirit of the enslaved and slaughters the conscience of the enslaver. . . .*

50

Suddenly she realized a shadow had fallen over the pages in front of her. Startled, she gasped and looked up. "Jess!" She clambered up from the floor, dropping the book and almost tipping over the candle.

His face bore the strain of a long, tiring day, and fatigue was clearly etched in the lines webbing out from his eyes. "I'm sorry, I didn't mean to frighten you. For heaven's sake, Kerry, what are you doing on the floor?" He shook his head in exasperation, watching her replace the candle on his desk.

"What are you reading?" He reached down to retrieve the book she'd dropped, one eyebrow arching with surprise and a slow smile playing at the corners of his mouth.

"Heavy stuff for such a small girl, isn't it?" He loosened his collar and draped his coat over the desk chair.

"I—I just wanted something to read, and I saw this on the shelf and—"

"Well, you're welcome to read it, of course," he said quickly. "But there are far more interesting books in here, I assure you." He rubbed his hands together and knelt in front of the fireplace, setting another log on the fire and stoking it gently until it caught. Confident the fire would blaze for a while, he lowered himself wearily onto the ginger-colored settee, motioning Kerry to come sit beside him.

"Sit down, Kerry—I want to talk with you."

She sat down uncertainly and huddled against the far end of the settee, staring into the fire while she kept as much distance as possible between them.

"Uh-oh, what's this? Are you still angry with me?"

"No!" she protested, not very convincingly.

"I think you are," he sighed. "And you have reason to be. Kerry—look at me." When she hesitated, he moved closer to her. "Please—*look* at me."

Reluctantly, she complied, her irritation with him wavering when she saw the apology reflected in his tender blue

51

gaze. She blinked and swallowed hard, fighting the unbidden desire to move even closer to him.

"Have you forgiven me?" he asked softly.

Knowing what he meant, she nodded, looking away from him.

"Kerry, I wasn't angry with you. I was shocked—and furious with Martin. I never dreamed he'd try such a thing. Surely you know I wouldn't have sent you with him if I had even suspected he was . . . that sort of man."

His nearness and the intensity of his searching gaze assailed her with turbulent feelings. She tried to keep her voice calm, but she was sure he could sense her turmoil. "It's all right, Jess, I understand. Truly I do."

"Well, you'll be glad to know he won't bother you again; he's gone."

"What do you mean?"

"He was dismissed a short while ago. He already had nearly two hundred demerits, you see; it was just a matter of time. I only wish his finish hadn't come at your expense."

"What are demerits?"

"They're marks against a man. Each cadet is required to adhere to a code of honor. When that code is breached, demerits are issued, two hundred bringing an automatic dismissal. So, you see, Martin was close to being dismissed even before this afternoon."

"What is this—code of honor? A rule book?"

"No, it's not in a book. A cadet is on his honor not to cheat or lie or steal—nor to tolerate it in another cadet. The whole system here at the Academy is based upon truth and the honor of a man."

"You mean that every man is responsible for himself?"

"Exactly. And it works, although that often surprises civilians."

His smile created in her that strange mixture of pleasure

and uneasiness that occurred more and more frequently each time she was close to him. She was uncomfortably aware of the large amount of space he seemed to occupy, and her pulse went wild when he reached for her hands and grasped both of them in his.

"Kerry . . . what I said to you this afternoon, about staying away from the cadets . . . I was—upset. I didn't mean it the way it may have sounded to you."

When she didn't answer, he gently framed her face between his large hands, forcing her to look at him. "Kerry?"

His tenderness moved her like a caress. Still, knowing his innate kindness and peculiar sensitivity for the feelings of those around him, she tried not to make too much of it. *He'd give any small thing he felt sorry for the same look,* she told herself firmly. *It isn't that I'm special to him, no more so than a bothersome younger sister would be.* But if that were true, why did his next murmured words cause such a warm glow to envelop her?

"Do you understand that I care about you, dear? That you're important to me?"

Her gaze slid over the silken thickness of his dark beard, lingering on the firmly molded mouth. He was so close she could feel his soft breath upon her cheek, and she was certain he could see her pulse pounding at her throat. *I wish . . . oh, what would it be like, being wrapped in those strong arms of his? If only he would hold me, just hold me, even for a moment . . . I could make that last a long, long time. Oh, whatever am I thinking? Sure, and he'd have a good laugh if he knew the foolishness going through my mind, and him thinking I'm no more than an annoying child.*

Something in the combination of her impossible imaginings and Jess's gentle kindness triggered the fleeting image of Lowell Martin's mocking face, causing her to pull in a shaky breath in an effort to subdue the sudden trembling that threatened to overtake her. For one terrible moment she thought she was going to be ill. She turned abruptly away from Jess, hugging her arms tightly to her body.

But he had seen the lightning-fast change wash over her face. He reacted immediately, closing the small distance between them as he gathered her into the warm circle of his arms and coaxed her head onto his chest.

Kerry knew she should move away, but the wonder of having her irrational longings fulfilled held her captive as she gave herself up to the safe comfort of his shoulder.

"Kerry, what is it, dear? What's wrong?" he asked softly, his voice edged with concern.

She shook her head, unable to speak, fighting back the tears. *I must not cry . . . I never cry . . . I'll not have him thinking I'm more of a child than he already believes me to be. . . .*

"Kerry, did Martin . . . did he hurt you more than you've told Molly or me?"

"No, Jess, it was nothing like that," she answered miserably. "I'm being foolish, I know," she stammered. His embrace tightened somewhat as though to reassure her. "It wasn't . . . so much what he did, you see, as what he said."

"What did he say, Kerry? Tell me, dear," he insisted, his hand pressing her head firmly against him.

The tears came now, in spite of her determination to contain them. "He—he said it wasn't as though I were a—a *lady!*" Her face heated with color at the renewed memory of the afternoon. "He made me feel as though it didn't matter at all to him what he did to me—simply because of who I am."

She felt his heartbeat accelerate against her cheek, heard his sharp intake of breath as he tightened his protective hold on her even more. "Kerry, it's not an easy thing to understand, I know, but you must realize that there are those people who attack whatever is foreign to them, what-

54

ever is different. Fortunately, we don't get many of that sort here at the Academy. But Lowell Martin is a product of grossly wealthy parents who spoiled and coddled him right into a conscienceless state of supreme selfishness. Nothing seems to be sacred to him except his own wants and needs. He's a totally self-centered boy who views everyone else as no more than instruments of his bidding. I pray God you won't meet many like him but when you do, try to remember that you're dealing with ignorance. Don't ever, ever let them influence the way you feel about yourself."

She heard the anger in his tone and wondered uneasily if any of it were directed at her. Did he think her responsible at all for the incident? "I am sorry, Jess, for the trouble this has been to you."

He put her gently away from him, holding her by the shoulders as he searched her gaze. "Don't you ever blame yourself for what happened today, Kerry. It's over, and I want your promise to forget it."

Silently she told herself it would be a very long time indeed before she would be able to dismiss the memory of Cadet Martin's contempt, but she simply nodded and replied, "Aye, Jess."

Finally releasing her from his embrace, he patted her shoulder rather awkwardly and rose from the settee. "There's something else I've been wanting to discuss with you," he said casually. He walked over to the fireplace and began stoking the dying embers back to life.

"I've noticed that you seem to be somewhat bothered about your lack of formal education. Am I right, Kerry?"

"I—how did you know that?" *Wasn't he the most remarkable man, though? At times he seemed to read her mind, he did!*

Returning to the settee, he shrugged, smiling at her. "I don't know; I suppose it's something I've sensed. How would you like to do something about it?"

"What d'you mean? Whatever could I do about it?"

He stood looking down at her for a moment, pushing the sleeves of his shirt up above his muscled forearms. "I'm a teacher, too, you know—not just a preacher."

"Oh, yes. I know that," she declared, her eyes sparkling with admiration. "And a writer as well. Molly says you're a famous man."

With a wry grin, he sat down by her again, leaning forward with his hands clasped together. "Don't put too much stock in what Molly says. She tends to be a bit prejudiced about me at times. Anyway, how would you like to be my own private student? Let me tutor you in some of the subjects you're interested in. We'd have most evenings together, and you'd have some time throughout the day to study when you're not helping Molly. Would you like to try that?"

She looked at him doubtfully, trying to suppress the excitement racing through her. "You're not serious, surely? I mean, why would you—"

He reached out and ruffled her hair. "Let's just say I'd welcome a bit of variety, all right? I get tired of staring at all those long, military faces."

"You're teasing me now, and I never know what to make of you when you do that."

Immediately contrite, he protested, "I wouldn't tease about something like this, dear. Tell me, now, what would you like to learn about, more than anything else?"

"You *are* serious!" Her heart raced. To have the chance to learn—really *learn*—with a man as brilliant as Jess, sure and it was more than she could have ever dreamed of. Perhaps, if she learned quickly and well, he'd come to see her as a young woman rather than an ignorant child.

A warm gleam rose in his eyes as he saw her enthusiasm. "I've never been more serious, Kerry. Now then, tell me—do you have a particular choice of subject you'd like to concentrate on first?"

She thought for only an instant. "Aye, that I do. I want to study America."

Tracing his mustache with his index finger, he said thoughtfully, "You mean history?"

"Everything," she breathed fervently. "I want to learn everything there is to know about this country, right from the beginning."

"Well, you've certainly chosen a subject dear to my heart. Tell me something, Kerry, do you have a special reason for wanting to learn more about your new country?"

She considered his question carefully before replying. "Because it *is* my country, first of all. And because it's all so confusing, these United States."

"Confusing? What do you mean?"

"Well, it seems to be like a giant puzzle, I'm thinking . . . so many separate states, and each of them different. Some appear to be peaceable, but others like to spat . . . some believe in owning people as slaves, while others do not . . . some are like enormous farms, while others are mostly cities and factories. It's as though each fits together, but at the same time no one is like the other. If I'm to be living here," she said soberly, "I want to try to understand the people. I cannot do that, now can I, unless I know about their beginnings, their hopes and dreams, and such?"

Surprised and pleased at the perception of this child-woman who sat next to him looking into his eyes with ingenuous excitement, Jess felt a thrill of anticipation he hadn't felt for years. "I think," he said softly, "you already know far more about America than some of us who were born within her shores, Kerry. In fact, I believe you could teach me a few things."

She flushed at his praise. "You'll be finding out how much I *don't* know, I'm afraid," she murmured, searching his face for any hint of condescension.

"What you don't know isn't important, Kerry—only what you'll learn." He covered her hand with his. "Anyway, you mustn't mind my discovering those things you need to learn. That's not a weakness, you see. Being honest enough to admit what you don't know is actually a strength."

"Then you truly do mean it—about the lessons?"

Giving her an exasperated grin, he tapped her playfully on the end of her nose with one finger. "Yes, Kerry Shannon, I mean it. But if you doubt my word once more, I may just change my mind."

"Oh, Jess," she exclaimed, her voice catching with emotion, "I'll work so hard!"

He nodded, squeezing her hand. "Yes, I know you will." Rising from the settee, he pulled her to her feet. "Now then, I want you to go upstairs and get a good night's rest. You've had a long and very difficult day. I want you fresh when we begin our studies tomorrow.

He brushed the top of her head with a gentle, brotherly kiss. When his hands lingered lightly on her shoulders as he turned her toward the door, she decided that this entire evening had been a wonder, and that was the truth.

He watched her, smiling at the way her slight figure appeared to bounce with energy as she ran up the stairs. *Ah, Kerry, Kerry, what are you doing to me? Why does my world seem to be shining night and day since you've become a part of it?*

CHAPTER SIX

During the next few weeks, Kerry and Jess fell into an evening routine of leisurely walks and hours of study. The sunset parade was a regular part of their time together, a breathtaking spectacle that never failed to stir Kerry. The precision marching of the cadets, their shouldered bayonets reflecting the blazing glints from the setting sun, their hat plumes waving in the cold, autumn breeze, and the cadence of the drums gave the scene a daily freshness. For Kerry it was a continual source of inspiration, and for Jess, a constant source of pleasure to see her eyes shine with excitement as they stood, side by side beneath the sunset.

Molly would occasionally serve them an early supper when Jess had evening duties, but more often they had a late meal after the parade, then went off to Jess's study for an hour or two of tutoring.

Kerry anticipated their study time with all the eagerness

of a hungry child getting ready for a feast. But she soon discovered that for a man who possessed such a kind heart and a generous spirit, Jess Dalton wore a robe of a different color as an instructor.

It seemed to Kerry that the more she accomplished, the more he expected. She loved the work and thrived on the challenge. Jess occasionally commented on her progress. Most of the time, however, he was relentless in pushing her further. He insisted that she accept nothing as it appeared to be, but form her own conclusions after sifting through and categorizing her facts. Even then he would question her unmercifully to make her support her answers. His praise was infrequent and never effusive.

"The man is never satisfied," she complained to Molly. The two of them were putting the finishing touches on the mince pies they were preparing for the next day's Thanksgiving dinner. "Sure, and he must know how hard I study, yet he seldom gives me so much as an encouraging nod. But he's quick enough to tell me when I'm wrong, he is."

"Would you be telling me, lass, what might be so urgent about all this book learning? It'll not be making you a better wife or mother, will it now?" Molly snapped impatiently as she moved the pies to the cupboard shelf. "Ach, I should not have let you talk me into making these pies a day ahead. I'll be fretting all day that they'll be stale.

"A few hours won't be making a bit of difference in the pies, Molly. You'll be glad you did it this way, just see if you're not." Irritated, Kerry gave the nearby woodbox a sharp kick, then slammed a pan of water down on the stove with a resounding clang.

"Might it not be, Molly—to answer your question—that a lass could be interested in something more than merely preparing herself to take care of a man for the rest of her life?"

"Such as?" Molly wiped her hands on her yellow-checked

apron with a derisive sniff.

"Such as learning about the world, perhaps."

"Aye, learning is a fine thing if one knows what they will be doing with it," the housekeeper said pointedly.

"What I intend to do with it is to be a lady—just as fine a lady as . . . ."

She broke off her retort when she heard the faint whistle outside that always heralded Jess's arrival. She forced her anger into a tight-lipped smile of greeting as he came through the door, stamping from his boots the residue of light snow which had begun to fall earlier. Kerry thawed considerably as soon as he smiled. It wasn't his fault, after all, that his housekeeper was so thickheaded.

"Missed you on our walk this evening, Kerry," he said, tossing his heavy black greatcoat over the wall hook, then dabbing the snowflakes away from his beard. "It's snowing harder now."

When she didn't answer, he continued. "Well, I'll go on to the study to read until you're done here." The look he gave her before he left the room plainly said that he was puzzled by her unusual solemnness.

Neither Molly nor Kerry spoke for quite some time after Jess had gone, although they continued to work together. Finally, having enough of the strained silence, Kerry decided to change the subject. Besides, there was a question she had wanted to ask Molly for weeks now.

"Molly—might I ask . . . were you ever married?"

With a sharp glance, Molly lifted an inquiring brow, flapped her apron a few times, then grabbed the broom and began to briskly sweep the kitchen floor. "Aye, I was. Not for long—but I was married once."

Kerry waited, beginning to think there would be no more information forthcoming. Surprised, she saw a rare tear cloud the housekeeper's eyes as she leaned a moment on her broom.

"He died, you see. Little more than a year after we arrived in America."

"Oh—I'm so sorry, Molly. What was your husband like? Did you love him very much?"

"Humph!" Molly reddened. "When I was a lass, there was a bit more to love than what's meant today. But he was a good man, Patrick was, a few years older than I, even-tempered, hardworking, and honest as a saint." Her voice softened, and her eyes held a smile when she added, "Yes . . . I loved him."

"You said he was older than you?"

"A few years, not that it mattered."

"It made no difference?" Kerry asked casually.

"Not that I ever knew," she replied. "With some it does, with others it doesn't, I should think."

"Aye," Kerry murmured distractedly. A new thought occurred to her. "Have you children, Molly?"

"None but you and our Jess—and that's more than enough worry, I'm sure!" She attempted a stern frown, straightening her back to a ramrod stiffness. "Get on with you, now. You'll be of no use to me the rest of this evening, knowing he's waiting in the study. Go along, get to your learning."

"I should have thought you'd be pleased about my studies, Molly," Kerry said defensively. "Instead, all you do is poke fun at me."

"It's not fun I'm making, lass," Molly replied, mellowing somewhat. "You've a good mind, our Jess says, and I'm thinking it's fine that you want to learn. But it's another hunger I've seen growing in you that bothers me a bit, and all the learning within your reach will not erase it, I can tell you."

"Whatever are you talking about?"

"Knowledge of the books won't be making you a lady, Miss. And even if it would, you'd not be feeling any better about yourself until you learn to be content as the good Lord made you."

Kerry tapped her foot impatiently. "If you're trying to tell me something, Molly Larkin, I wish you'd just get on with it."

"I am trying to tell you, lass, that you won't be changing your opinion of yourself—or our Jess's estimation of you, either—with a world of learning. The things that make a slip of a girl a lady are not to be found between the covers of any book."

"I couldn't be caring any less about what *our Jess* thinks of me. He's made it quite clear that I'm not to be considered a woman grown, and it would seem that you agree with him—as you always do!" Tearing off her white pinafore apron and flinging it onto a chair, Kerry hiked up the waistline of her brown wool skirt and flounced out of the kitchen.

Jess caught a glimpse of her whisking by his study and, rising from his desk chair, called out to her. "Kerry? Where are you going?"

She stopped just past the door and drew a long breath. "I'm not feeling like studying tonight, I'm afraid. I'll just be going to bed, if that's all right," she answered shortly.

He appeared at the open door, a concerned look on his face. "You're not ill, are you?" He'd changed into a soft flannel shirt as blue as his eyes, and she felt an unwelcome wave of fondness for him sweep over her.

"No—I'm simply tired, and as Molly's been kind enough to remind me, all this studying is no more than a waste of time anyway, so I'll—"

"Whoa, whoa—wait a minute!" He caught her by the forearm and led her into the study. "Now, what's this about Molly? The two of you aren't arguing, are you?"

"Oh, never mind! It doesn't make a bit of difference,

anyway. She's right. You can't be making a silk purse out of a sow's ear, now can you?"

Ignoring her efforts to pull away from him, he demanded, "Would you like to tell me why you're so angry?"

"I am not angry! I simply want to be left alone. I've had a stomach full of being treated like a—a mindless infant!"

"Then stop acting like one!" he retorted impatiently, turning around to shut the study door. "Now . . . suppose you sit down and tell me what has you so upset."

She tried to wriggle out of his grasp, but her effort was almost laughable. Glaring defiantly, she stood still as a statue, refusing to utter a word.

With deliberate patience, he pleaded gently, "Kerry—sit down and talk with me."

Lifting her chin belligerently, she replied, "I don't want to sit down."

"Whatever are we going to do with that temper of yours, little one? Come on now, tell me what's wrong." He loosened his grip slightly, but not enough for her to move away.

With an exaggerated sigh, she said, very precisely, "I am tired of your treating me as though I'm no more than a babe in dydees. And I am tired of Molly's telling me how I'm wasting my time—and yours—with all this studying, and how I won't be needing it because I'm *only* going to be a wife and mother!"

He felt an unexpected stab of pain at her reference to marriage. The thought of her belonging to another man was repugnant to him. He knew his reaction was selfish. Of course, she would need a young man to spend her life with—she couldn't stay with him and Molly forever. Still, the thought of her in the arms of another man caused an overwhelming surge of denial to course through him.

Because she obviously expected some sort of reply from him, he began, faltering for an instant, "You might try to be a little more understanding with Molly. She truly cares for you, you know; she's only concerned for your welfare."

Her flushed cheeks darkened even more. "Well, if you agree with her, just why are you wasting your precious time on me?"

"You know I don't think of it as a waste of time. You *are* being childish now."

He looked . . . pompous . . . yes, pompous, she decided with exasperation. "Oh, stop it! Just stop it!"

"Stop what?" He drew back from her, momentarily bewildered.

"Stop pat—pat—" Her voice caught in frustration. "Whatever that word is."

"Patronizing? You think I'm patronizing you? No, Kerry—"

"What you're doing is making fun of me." Unwelcome tears, which always seemed to come when she was angry, began to burn her eyes.

"Kerry, dear . . . ."

She pushed blindly at his chest with her fists, humiliated that she'd allowed herself to completely lose her composure with him. *He said I was being childish—and I am.*

"I didn't mean to hurt you, Kerry; I wouldn't. Surely you know that. And Molly wouldn't either, dear, never deliberately—"

"There you go again. *Dear!* Oh. I hate it when you do that, when you treat me as though I'm but a difficult child—I hate it! You and Molly both—you think I'm so amusing, don't you?"

He caught his breath in surprise, still baffled by her anger. But he saw something else in her eyes—humiliation? It tugged at his heart. His voice was little more than a whisper when he answered, "I'd never make fun of you, Kerry—don't you know that?"

Slowly, hesitantly, he gathered her in his arms, gently cushioning her head against the broad expanse of his chest.

Kerry's senses exploded when she felt his heart thud against her cheek. She clung to him as though she were falling, closing her eyes against the dizzying rotation of the room, holding her breath as his lips hesitantly brushed her forehead.

She raised her eyes slowly upward to lock for an instant with his stunned, wondering gaze. He was staring down at her as though he'd never seen her before. Breathless, she watched him study her face with a look of discovery and a tenderness that made her heart squeeze with anticipation. It seemed so very right, the most natural thing in the world, that he would lower his lips to hers in a kiss so gentle, so wonderfully sweet that Kerry thought she surely must be dreaming.

The kiss lasted only a moment, but she knew it would change her life forever. He sighed softly and murmured her name against the thick cascade of flossy curls at her temple. She felt his strong, sure hands tremble on her shoulders, and she feared she would cry out with the swift flood of joy that threatened to overwhelm her senses.

Then she saw the stricken look of regret upon Jess's face.

Horror glazed his features as he pushed her, almost roughly, away from him. "Kerry—" His voice was no more than a hoarse whisper. "Forgive me. I'm so sorry . . . ." Even as guilt struck him full force, his reason drowned in the glory of the caress that had been his—if only for a moment. Drawing from the deepest reservoir of self-control he possessed, he shook off his entrancement and mentally scourged himself. *She's but a child, man. And your ward, at that!*

66

But he knew he lied to himself as he stood there, his arms still outstretched as though to hold her safely at bay. The child who had come to them from Buffalo now stood poised on the threshold of womanhood, adorned with the promise of an exquisite, heartrending loveliness.

He had tried to make her a little sister, a charming pet, an object of safe affection. In doing so he had allowed his fondness free reign, unmindful until now of the change the weeks had wrought in her. A steady diet of wholesome food, exercise, and relief from the drain of poverty's bondage had added an enchanting feminine softness to her once slight figure and colored her fair skin with a zest for life. Her hair was a tumble of copper fire, and her emerald eyes had captured sunbeams for their own special light.

Like a fool, he had allowed his protective instinct for the girl to grow unchecked, and his original innocent desire to cherish her, which had motivated him from the very beginning, now threatened to burst into a forbidden emotion. Staring down into her bewildered, waiting eyes, he realized she might feel obligated to bend to whatever relationship he chose to foster because of her situation. Surely his sanity had deserted him, causing him to lose his grip on reality. And now he must undo this—he *must*.

"I'm sorry," he whispered again, moving even farther back from her.

"No, Jess—oh, don't be sorry." Her voice caught as the words spilled from her.

When she would have moved closer to him once more, he stopped her. He grasped her firmly on the shoulder with one hand and laid the fingers of his other hand lightly over her lips. "You must forget this, Kerry. I had no right . . . ."

She looked as though he had struck him. "But didn't you want to kiss me, Jess? Did I do something wrong . . . ?" Her whispered question trailed off, faltering when his wounded gaze burned into her.

67

"*No,* Kerry! You did nothing wrong—I'm the one at fault. I should never have allowed it to happen."

Dismayed, he saw the pained confusion in her eyes. *She thought he was rejecting her.* Anxious to make her understand, yet despairing of a way to do so without making the situation worse, he nearly groaned aloud with frustration. "Kerry—listen to me, please. I—forgot for a moment that I'm your guardian. That was wrong of me. I meant only to comfort you, not . . . ."

He saw the doubt in her eyes and knew he was only making things worse. Furious with himself, he tried once more to undo the consequences of his rashness. "Fourteen years, Kerry—that's a great difference. And even if it weren't so great, I'm still responsible for you—you're my ward, after all." He twisted his mouth in self-mockery. "Everything I do is supposed to be in your best interests. This is hardly," he muttered harshly, "to your benefit."

His face was contorted with regret as he tightened his grip on her small shoulders. "I want you to promise me you'll forget all about this. I assure you it will never happen again."

When she remained silent, he prompted sternly, "Kerry? Do you understand?"

Her voice thickened as she dropped her gaze to the floor. "Of course, I understand. And if you can forget it so easily, you needn't worry yourself that I'll be giving it any thought. It was just a kiss, after all."

Somewhat relieved, he nodded uncertainly, releasing her from his grasp. "Well—you'd best go on to bed now. The Superintendent and his wife will be here for an early Thanksgiving dinner tomorrow. Molly's going to need your help first thing in the morning, I'm sure." Turning away from her, he walked stiffly toward the fireplace.

An ache twisted her heart when she saw the unhappy

slump of his broad shoulders. But it failed to stop her retort. "Whatever you say, sir."

Long after midnight, Kerry was still making a futile attempt to forget the feel of Jess's arms around her and the sweetness of his mouth upon hers. Finally, tired of thrashing about beneath the voluminous quilts Molly insisted upon piling on her, she slipped out of bed, pulled on her much-worn flannel bathrobe, and curled up on the window seat, hugging her knees close to her chin.

The ground beneath her window was beginning to look like white velvet under the still falling snow. A sharp western wind picked up a drift and slammed it harshly against the gatepost. She shivered as though she, too, had been hit by the same cold blast.

How could she have allowed herself to imagine, even for a moment, that Jess had kissed her because he was coming to care for her as a woman? And what had he thought of her behavior once his head had cleared?

But what *had* moved him to kiss her? It certainly had not been her idea. Not that she hadn't enjoyed it, she admitted . . . *I wonder if he could tell it was my first kiss? Though I'm certain it wasn't his . . . he was engaged, after all.* Not wanting to think about that—refusing to, in fact—she returned to her puzzling about his motivation.

Ninny! He's a man, is he not? And a lonely man, if I'm not too badly mistaken. Even a strong man such as Jess can be tempted by a female who's locked up with him evening after evening, especially when there are no others about under the age of fifty.

You might just as well admit it, Kerry O'Neill: You let your imagination run wild, is what you did. Jess might like you well enough as a "little sister," and he might have been carried away with his emotions for a bit—didn't Da warn you about the natural passions of men?—but don't go making more of it than it was.

His one true love was a real lady, you must remember, a lady of good family and education and—yes, the right age as well. You'd do well, lassie, not to forget that in the old country you'd be cleaning privies and scrubbing floors for such a family as the Daltons or his fine lady Emily. Molly's right: You need to be accepting things as God made them and be content, instead of sitting around dreaming foolish dreams about a man who'd never touch you when he's at himself. And if you'd be needing any further proof, mind the way he backed off from you once he came to his senses—as though he'd been burned by a scoop of hot coals!

Not until she grew so cold that she could no longer bear it did she return to her bed. Her restless tumbling of the earlier hours continued until she saw the first pale hint of dawn creep through her window. And though she finally slept, she could get no rest among the puzzling, agitated images that webbed the pathway of her dreams.

CHAPTER SEVEN

Jess was polite but distant throughout Thanksgiving Day, a pattern that repeated itself during the following week. Kerry tried not to mind but, in truth, his withdrawal left her desolate.

Frustrated by the total helplessness of her situation, she watched him retreat and grieved that she had become such a problem to him. For her part, she'd not be forgetting the wonder of being in his arms, even for those brief, fleeting moments. But for Jess, she wished there were a way to pretend it had never happened.

She firmly resolved that if he wanted to be no more than a kindly older brother to her, then she in turn would be no more than a well-behaved younger sister to him. Adopting a sweet, polite manner toward him, she followed his lead in keeping their conversation light, friendly, and meaningless.

She was greatly relieved after a few days when she

detected a slight thaw in his coolness. Anxious not to displease him, she groped carefully for her answer when he asked if she'd be interested in attending a chamber music concert in honor of a visiting German duke. He explained that Cadet Edmund Teague had requested permission to escort her. For a moment, she believed he wanted and expected her to accept the cadet's invitation. But once she did, she was troubled by a glint of something unpleasant in his gaze. However, it quickly passed, and she told herself it must have been her imagination. Jess would hardly care one way or the other whether she went to a concert.

The following week brought another surprise. Jess appeared late one afternoon after a mysterious two-day absence. He had enough material for at least half a dozen different dresses, including one lovely piece of light green silk. He instructed Molly to make it into a formal gown for the concert.

When Kerry would have protested his extravagance on her behalf, he dismissed her objections easily. "Kerry, you've needed a new wardrobe for some time. Since you cannot attend a concert without proper apparel—and you did say you wanted to go, now didn't you?—I decided this was a convenient time to do some shopping for you."

His voice fell and his face reddened somewhat as he continued. "You'll. . . ah. . . find some other packages in your room. I—took the liberty of making a few additional purchases I thought you might need. Molly helped me with a list."

Too excited to argue further, Kerry rushed upstairs to her room with Molly close behind her. She found the bed heaped with packages from a variety of shops in New York City. The wrappings yielded a breathtaking assortment of feminine treasures, including delicate lingerie. A warm blush flooded her cheeks. She turned questioning eyes to Molly, who quickly reassured her in her matter-of-fact fashion.

"Don't be looking so fierce now, Miss. Jess knew what you had need of because I informed him. His Aunt Marian, his mother's sister, selected the more intimate items. It was all quite proper, never fear."

She immediately fell to helping Kerry put everything away. "I'll have the dress for your concert made up well ahead of time, just as Jess wants. It'll be lovely, that pale green with your hair. Run along now—I'll finish this. You'll be wanting to thank your Jess, I'm sure."

She found him in the entryway, shrugging into his black greatcoat and about to go out the door. Suddenly overwhelmed by the extent of his kindness to her, she felt strangely shy as she approached him.

"Jess?" He waited, looking down at her with an affectionate smile.

"I—I wanted to thank you. It's all so lovely—truly lovely. But you shouldn't have bought me so much. I don't need all those pretty things."

He reached out to gently tug at a rebellious auburn curl. "You deserve pretty things, Kerry. And I have no one else to buy them for, after all. Let me do this for you, dear—I enjoy it." His voice was wonderfully tender, his gaze like a warm touch.

Oh, what a puzzle he was. He could make her shiver with his indifference one moment and melt her with his sweet kindness in another. Sometimes she felt as though her world were constantly tilting, and she never knew which way she'd come up next.

When Kerry came gliding down the stairs the night of the concert, she found both Edmund and Jess waiting for her. She caught herself seeking Jess's approval first, and her heart turned over when she saw his intense blue gaze sweep over her with obvious admiration.

Molly, as adept with a needle as with a recipe, had created

a masterpiece from the pale green silk. The fitted bodice fell in deep points over a single skirt decorated in satin braid. The neckline was cut straight across with just a slight dip in front, with folds of material arranged *a la grecque*. An elegant white evening drapery covered the short sleeves. To Kerry's delight, Jess had even thought of dainty white silk boots to complete the outfit.

At the first glimpse of herself in the upstairs mirror, she'd been jolted by the image staring back at her. She felt as though she were outside her own body, watching a stranger pirouette about the room. She stopped every few seconds to peer again at her reflection, finally smiling with amazed pleasure.

Now, she hesitated at the bottom of the stairway as Edmund approached her, a flattering smile brightening his mischievous features. Jess stood large and solemn behind the cadet, and Kerry wondered what her guardian was thinking.

She would have been astonished had she known the havoc her appearance was wreaking upon his already turbulent emotions. He found the young woman before him almost frightening. *What a vision she is,* he thought, unable to stop his heart from wrenching when Teague took her arm.

The unbidden stab of jealousy reminded him that his response to the girl was to be no more than brotherly affection. He resolutely turned his attention to the cadet, who was openly admiring Kerry with fascination.

"Mr. Teague?"

"Sir?" Edmund reluctantly transferred his gaze to the chaplain.

"I can trust you to have Miss O'Neill back inside this door no later than eleven this evening, can I not?"

"Yes, sir! Not a minute later, Mr. Dalton, sir."

74

Had he not felt quite so irritable—or so *old*—Jess would have been amused at the two of them. Kerry, who had never been to a concert in her life, was fairly bouncing with enthusiasm. Bless her, she might never be altogether *proper*—somehow he hoped she wouldn't—but she was incredibly lovely. And Teague—*young* Teague, he repeated to himself with vexation—was about to swallow his tongue if he didn't catch some air soon. But who could blame the boy? She was enough to take any man's breath away.

Kerry was surprised to see Jess walk in just before the beginning of the concert; he hadn't even mentioned to her that he'd be attending. But there he was, splendid in his black, swallowtail dress coat with the high collar and wide cravat. His hair was still a bit undisciplined, as it always was, but this trait only endeared him to her that much more. She decided he was the most handsome man there, in spite of the fact that he looked slightly uncomfortable in his fancy evening clothes.

He made his way to her during the intermission; Edmund had gone to get some punch for them, and Kerry was standing close to the wall, looking lost and uneasy amidst the crowd of cadets and visiting dignitaries.

"And why did you not tell me you were going to be here tonight, Jess?" Her eyes brightened with pleasure as he approached.

He shrugged, giving her an easy smile. "I didn't really decide I was coming until the last minute. I'm not much for chamber music, as a rule. Are you enjoying it?"

"Oh, my, yes! Especially that last selection, the one with the flute. Wasn't it lovely?"

He smiled down at her. "Ah, yes, I'd almost forgotten—your father played the flute, didn't he?"

"And so did I, once," she offered shyly.

"Kerry, you never told me that before. Where's your

flute? Do you still have it?"

"No—it was Da's. A short while before he died he took it to a place where they repaired such things. There was something wrong with it, you see." She attempted an indifferent shrug, but her misty eyes betrayed her. "After he died, I was never able to find out where it was. Besides, I probably would not have been able to pay the cost."

"I'm sorry, dear," he said softly, studying her face tenderly. As Edmund returned with the punch, Jess turned his gaze from Kerry and glanced idly about the room as he engaged both of them in a few minutes of small talk.

"He's an unusual man, isn't he?" Edmund asked casually after Jess had returned to his chair several rows away.

"What? Oh—yes, he is." Kerry quickly returned her attention to the cadet.

"I suppose he's very good to you." It was more a statement than a question, and he continued before she had a chance to answer. "Most of the men think he's fine, even though some of the bigwigs would occasionally like to hang him."

Kerry turned alarmed eyes on the cadet. "Whatever do you mean?"

He shrugged, taking another drink of punch before replying. "He's a bit—controversial, you see. Not everyone shares his feelings about equality, you can be sure of that. For myself, I think he's an inspiring man. You're fortunate to be around him so much."

Not replying to his last statement, Kerry set her half-full punch cup down on a nearby table. *Fortunate?* she mused, accompanying him back to their chairs. *I wonder . . . I'm thinking it only makes everything harder, trying not to care so much for him, yet having to see him, to be near him, every day. . . .*

By the time she and Edmund arrived at the gate after the concert, Kerry was laughing with delight at the cadet's outlandish stories about his family—apparently a large, rather uninhibited tribe who had little use for convention or the rules of society. Kerry wasn't surprised that Edmund came from an unpretentious background, though not so poor as her own. She'd detected a kindred spirit in him right from the first and already liked him very much—as a friend.

Standing at the window of his study, Jess tightly clenched his hands behind his back as he watched the two young people come up the walk. He smiled a little at their laughter, at the same time rebuking himself for the jab of discomfort nagging at him. *Why shouldn't they like each other? Don't you want to see her happy—laughing and enjoying herself? She's had precious little merriment up to now. Ah, Lord . . . I do want her to be happy, of course. It's only that—well, the truth is, I suppose, that I wish I could be the one she laughs with, the one she smiles for.* He moved quickly away from the window when he saw them approach the porch steps.

A few moments later when Kerry entered the study, she found him standing before the hearth warming his hands.

"Jess? You left early. . . ."

"Mmm, I did." He had shed his dress coat and cravat for the comfort of an open collar and rolled-up shirtsleeves. "Well, I see Teague got you home just on time." He glanced at the shelf clock. "Did you enjoy the evening?"

"Oh, I did!" She hesitated uncertainly before adding, "I do want to thank you again, Jess—for the dress material and everything. I felt so grand tonight."

He said nothing for a time, then took a few steps toward her. "You couldn't possibly feel as grand as you look, dear."

The familiar, tender smile in his eyes blanketed her heart with a warm, sweet contentment. "Why, thank you, Jess. I—well, good night, then." But she made no move to leave the room.

He came closer, his hands knotting in large, tight fists, then opening again. "Kerry—" His voice was gentle but held an odd note of urgency.

"Yes, Jess?" Her reply was quick and breathless.

"I . . . ." He exhaled a deep, ragged sigh, his gaze never moving from her face. "Nothing. I'm glad you enjoyed your evening. I'll . . . see you in the morning." A non-commital mask cloaked his features.

Glancing over her shoulder just before she walked through the doorway, Kerry was bewildered by the peculiar stare etched on his face.

Why, Lord? Why do I seem to do nothing but upset him, when I want so very much to make him smile?

CHAPTER EIGHT

In the days following the concert, Kerry was relieved and somewhat surprised to see a return of the affection Jess had shown her during her first few weeks at West Point. His relaxed manner contributed to the easing of her own tension. With new zest, she threw herself into her studies, at the same time increasing her efforts to learn how to be a lady.

Jess was too sensitive not to notice. "Whatever happened to the little Irish spitfire who used to live here?" he teased one evening when she met him in the study with fresh coffee and an enormous piece of cake. He had just returned from calling on the Superintendent's wife, who was suffering from a violent bout with the grippe. "Who's this charming, well-mannered young lady I keep running into these days?" He loosened his collar, waiting for her to pour his coffee.

Knowing very well he was baiting her, Kerry wrinkled

her nose at him, presenting him with an exaggerated curt-sy and her thickest brogue. "Why, thank ye kindly, sir. I hope she's that pleasing to ye?"

He stared at her for a moment, saying nothing. She tried unsuccessfully to read his look of speculation, wondering if she'd said something to annoy him.

When he finally spoke, his voice was soft and his gaze as gentle as she'd even seen it. "She is . . . always very pleasing to me. Unfortunately, I sometimes fail to convey that fact." *And, unfortunately, I'm unable to deal with that fact. . . .*

Startled by his unexpected frankness, Kerry swallowed hard and attempted to lighten the moment as she set his coffee and cake on the desk. "And how did you find the Superintendent's wife this evening?"

He rolled up the sleeves of his white shirt and walked over to prod the logs on the fire into a higher blaze. "Not well, according to Dr. Greene. She's still carrying a danger-ously high fever. The family's very concerned."

"Aye, I should think so." She watched him, relishing the grace of his movements, unexpected in so large and pow-erful a man. She always enjoyed watching him and found pleasure in the things that seemed unique to Jess—his fine straight-backed walk and the endearing smile that made his eyes crinkle and her heart tumble.

He moved a chair close to his own at the desk and motioned for her to sit next to him. "This may be a long session," he warned her, referring to their study time. "We're going to talk about freedom of the press tonight. It's no easy feat to get me off that subject."

For several evenings he had been leading her, step by step, through the establishment of various freedoms in colonial America. Kerry had been as fascinated with the zeal and passion of his explanations as with the subjects themselves. Tonight was no exception. Once he'd finished his cake, he was up and about the room, pulling a variety of volumes from the shelves to illustrate his points as he came to them.

". . . So you see, the British arrested Zenger for criminal libel even though the only thing he was guilty of was criticizing the governor of New York. The poor man was left dangling; even his attorneys were disbarred. Under British law he was guilty, and that was that, no matter how factual his charges were."

"But what does this have to do with freedom of the press? You said his trial did nothing to change the law?"

"Ah—but the jury found him innocent, thanks to Andrew Hamilton. He was a famous Philadelphia lawyer who came to Zenger's aid. His defense was absolutely brilliant. Not only did he get Zenger acquitted, but the trial made people begin to think about the significance of all that was at stake." He replaced two of the larger books he'd taken down earlier. "It was a vital step toward making the public aware of the essential need for a free press, even though no laws were actually rewritten at the time. You see, dear, the first step in establishing any freedom is to convince people of the need for that freedom."

Standing in front of the drapery-covered window, he framed his face with the palms of both hands. Kerry smiled to herself, recognizing the familiar gesture as one that always preceded his attention drifting off to unknown places. Hoping to keep him with her for the moment, she asked quickly, "And that's what you're trying to do, isn't it, Jess? You're trying to make people see the need for freedom—for those with different-colored skin, such as the black people, and for those who are being taken advantage of by factory bosses and the like?"

He blinked, then gave her a vague smile. "Yes, I suppose that is what I'm trying to do, Kerry. But I'm only trying to make people listen to what God has already said. There's no

81

real choice about any of this. God never intended for us to enslave one another. In His eyes, there are no classes, no inferior citizens. We're all His children, and we're all free— free in Him."

She considered his words with a puzzled frown. "But we still have landowners and tenants, don't we, Jess? And nobles and commoners?"

He came to stand a few inches from her chair, looking down at her with a thoughtful expression. "That's the way of things in Ireland; that's what you're used to, isn't it?"

"Aye, it is. Some say it will be different one day, but I have my doubts about that. After all, there will always be the rich and the poor. What's to be done about it?"

"True," he agreed, "but that doesn't mean the rich should have license to rob the poor of their inherent rights, of their freedom." Continuing to study her, he leaned against the desk, crossing his arms over his chest. "You do understand, don't you, Kerry, that the worth of a person is endowed by God, not by another human being?"

She nodded uncertainly. "But it's also true, is it not, that our Lord has chosen to make some of His children wealthy and proper, while making others like me poor and igno- rant?" She watched him closely as he tapped his knuckles impatiently on the desk.

"You are *not* ignorant!" he flared. "You have a fine mind— a very bright mind, as a matter of fact." The truth was that he had found her to have a superior intelligence; she was alert, quick-witted, with a definite bent for history and the humani- ties. She was a joy to tutor, a once-in-a-lifetime student. "All right, you haven't had the advantage of a formal education. How long did you say you went to school in Ireland—six years?"

She nodded as he went on. "But you're doing something about that now, and you're doing it well, Kerry. Very well indeed." He saw her flush with pleasure and wondered

82

how she'd react if he were to tell her—as he longed to—how especially gifted he believed her to be. "And as for being poor—that's not true, either. You're a part of my family now," he said firmly. "A very . . . special part of it. Through no doing of my own, I have the means to take care of all of us—you, Molly, and myself—for as long as necessary, thank the Lord."

"But, Jess . . . ."

"Even if that weren't the case," he interrupted, "you wouldn't be poor. There's a poverty of spirit that has never touched you, Kerry. No, I suspect you have never really been poor," he said softly.

"Do you truly believe anything can ever be done about it—the divisions and classes and such?" she asked skeptically.

"There's much that can be done. From the pulpit, with a pen, in the legislature, the courts—the attitude that nothing can be done is the very reason so little *has* been done." His eyes smoldered with a fire she'd come to recognize by now.

"I have to believe that, Kerry, or my life is being spent for nothing. The men in my family have worked for freedom for generations. I'm simply carrying on what others began years and years before me."

"Like Mr. Andrew?" she prompted.

"Yes, certainly like my father," he agreed with a fond smile. "And his father. My grandfather spent a great many years working for the freedom of the vote. He was an attorney, too, but he was primarily a politician." His smile widened. "A very shrewd one, I'm told. He firmly believed the day would come—and so do I—when everyone, including women, will have the freedom to vote."

Kerry considered his words thoughtfully. "If I were to vote," she said very seriously, "I would vote only for those men who believe as you do, Jess."

He laughed, a rich rumble that started deep in his chest, a sound Kerry had grown to love and listen for. "There are those, my dear, who would use that statement as proof positive that a woman should never have the vote." His laughing eyes were warm with affection, and a sweet wave of joy coursed through her. She loved to make him smile, even more to make him laugh.

"I wonder, though," she said, sobering at the thought, "why is it that a wealthy man such as you is working so fiercely for others?" Fearing she might have overstepped her bounds, she added, "I'm sorry, Jess, I don't mean to be impertinent. But you are a famous man, a man of stature, Molly says. Why is it you care so much about the rights of others?"

"Because God cares," he answered deliberately. His heavy-lidded eyes darkened. "There is no justification—none—for one individual to deprive another of a freedom that's his according to the will of God."

Sensing that she was still doubtful, he attempted to clarify his feelings. "Kerry, freedom is like honor. It should never depend on wealth or education or skin color or on anything else. Just as honor is a state of the heart, freedom is a state of the soul. Do you understand what I'm saying?"

She nodded slowly. "Do you mean that people are honorable because of what's in their hearts rather than because of who they are? That money and education don't matter?"

"That's exactly what I mean," he declared eagerly. "Honor is between you and God. Of course, it eventually results in honorable relationships between you and others, but it begins with you and Him."

She grew quiet, needing to think about that. *If he's right, if all this is true, then I'm a person of worth after all!* She reasoned *Da was an honest, God-fearing man—poor as he was—and he raised me to be the same. Could this mean that my family is not to be scorned—nor am I? Could it mean that I might be good enough one day for Jess to . . . to love?* She caught her breath at the thought. *Provided, of course,* she quickly added to herself, *I could ever convince him that the years between us don't matter at all. . . .*

Suddenly aware that he was staring curiously at her, she forced her attention back to their conversation. "Why is it, Jess, that you became a chaplain rather than an attorney like your father and your grandfather?"

He locked his hands together and stretched his arms out in front of him for an instant, then walked around his desk. "I can only tell you that I knew, even when I was a boy, what God wanted me to do. I'm not exactly sure how I knew. I simply grew up with the conviction that I would serve Him in the pulpit and with a pen."

"But why did you choose to stay here at the Academy?"

He lifted his chin and she saw his eyes cloud with a far-away look. She had the strangest feeling that when he spoke he wasn't speaking to her alone. "Some of these young men," he said softly, "will one day be asked to lay down their lives for what they believe. Gentle, quiet men like Sam Grant, Tom Jackson, and others may eventually face a divided country and be required to fight for it—even to die for it."

He slowly walked over to the fireplace, his hands clasped behind his back. Once again, Kerry had the fleeting impression that he was sorely troubled in his spirit.

"What I want," he continued, "is for them to know what they believe in before they commit themselves to a country that may ask the ultimate sacrifice of them. I suppose, too, I like to think that the ideas I plant here in this remote place may travel with these men across the country and touch other lives as well."

He turned back to her with a gentle smile. "Where else could I have an opportunity like that? How else could I spread what I've believed in all my life so far, so quickly? For now at least, I believe God has called me to this place. Tomorrow . . . ." He shrugged lightly. "Tomorrow is also for Him to decide."

Both of them started with surprise when Molly stepped inside the doorway. "Jess, Edmund Teague is here, asking to see Kerry," she announced as she darted a questioning glance at the girl.

A quick look at Jess gave Kerry the uncomfortable feeling that he was displeased, but he said agreeably enough, "I see. Well, tell him to come in, Molly."

Disapproval shaded the housekeeper's reply. "He stated he would like to see her alone."

Kerry stood up quickly, casting a wide-eyed glance at Jess. "I—I'll just go and see what he wants," she offered hesitantly. "I'll be back in a moment, I'm sure." She hurried from the room, acutely aware that Jess's gaze followed her until she was out of sight.

CHAPTER NINE

Finding the cadet waiting in the hallway, Kerry exclaimed, "Edmund! Whatever are you doing here at this time of the night?"

He watched Molly make her way to the kitchen until she was out of sight. "It's all right, Kerry, I have permission to leave quarters. Listen," he said in a low, conspiratorial tone, "I need your help. Could you get some things from the kitchen for me? You know—a pan, some silverware, a couple of knives—that sort of stuff?"

"Whatever for?" she asked loudly.

He quickly shushed her, glancing furtively around the hall. "You wouldn't believe what they've been feeding us since Thanksgiving, Kerry. It's a crime. In self-defense, we've been carrying leftovers out of the mess in our caps for the past couple of days. Tonight we're going to have a hash, but we need some utensils. The ones we used last time have disappeared."

"A hash? What's a hash?" Kerry glared at him suspiciously.

"We cook whatever we can come up with over the fireplace in the room. Any leftovers you'd like to donate would be most appreciated!" He gave her an encouraging grin. "Come on, now, you'll help, won't you?"

"I most certainly will not," she retorted, posturing defiantly, her hands on her hips and one eyebrow lifted in reproach. "D'you have any idea at all what Molly Larkin would do to me were she to catch me taking utensils from her kitchen? You can just ask her yourself, Edmund Teague, if you're needing to borrow her things!"

"No!" he protested in a hoarse whisper. "Don't forget that Mr. Dalton is a part of the faculty. And cooking in the rooms is expressly forbidden. I've already got over 150 demerits—I surely can't afford any more." At a sign she was weakening, he pressed on. "I'm not asking you to steal, you know. I'll have everything back first thing tomorrow, I promise. Molly won't ever have to know about it. All we need are odds and ends—just a few— nothing important. Come on, now, Kerry, be a friend. Do you have any idea what it's like to be hungry?"

As if she could ever forget. She thought for a moment, sighed, gave him one more exasperated glare, then gave in. "All right; but you stay here for a bit. I'll have to talk Jess into letting me invite you in. If I'm to pass you the things you're needing, we'll have to get you into the kitchen somehow. And we'll certainly be needing to get rid of Molly."

Returning to the study, she found Jess engrossed in a new book that had arrived earlier in the week. She cleared her throat to get his attention, waiting for him to look up.

"Oh, you're back already? What was so urgent with Mr. Teague? Nothing's wrong, I hope?"

She bit her lower lip, feeling a terrible sense of guilt about what she was going to say. But still, it was to help a friend . . . .

88

"Oh, no, nothing's wrong! He just came to call a bit. Do you suppose I could ask him in for some refreshments? There's plenty of the coconut cake left." She watched him closely.

He studied her thoughtfully before answering. "Isn't it rather late?"

"Aye, but you know how these boys are always hungry, Jess. Wouldn't it be all right just this evening, since he's already here?"

He looked down at the page in front of him, and his reply was no more than a mumble. "I suppose it would be all right, just this once."

She waited, expecting him to say more. When he didn't speak again or look up at her, another stab of guilt prodded her. "You're—you're sure, then?"

His voice was firmer this time, almost impatient, but he kept his eyes on the book. "Yes, yes, go along."

Once she was out of the room, Jess scowled, irate at himself for being so short with her. He tried to be objective about the reason for his irritation. A wave of self-disgust engulfed him when he faced the truth. He leaned back in his chair, his eyes closed, and raked both hands down the sides of his face in a weary gesture.

It's only natural I know, Lord, for them to want to be together, he admitted to himself. *Why shouldn't she be interested in such a nice, good-looking cadet? Why wouldn't the boy want to be with her, lovely as she is? I can't expect her to prefer my company to his. I must seem dull and middle-aged to her in comparison to Teague. But it hurts, Lord . . . how it hurts. I know I cannot—I must not—care for her as I do. But how do I stop? How do I continue living in the same house, being close to her, longing to grow closer, yet knowing it can never be? Ah, Lord, have mercy, I beg You . . . deliver me from these hopeless feelings I have for the girl, please. . . .*

Molly predictably followed the two of them into the kitchen. Once Kerry explained that Jess had given permission for Edmund to stay, she insisted on cutting the cake and making fresh coffee. Casting a desperate glance at Edmund, Kerry grasped Molly firmly by the shoulders and began moving her toward the doorway. "No, Molly, you just go along and have yourself a bit of rest. I'm perfectly capable of fixing a bite to eat for Mr. Teague. We'll not be imposing upon your evening. Go on now."

Sighing with relief when the housekeeper finally left the kitchen and went upstairs to her room, Kerry cut a high, mouth-watering piece of coconut cake and set it in front of the cadet.

"I suppose," he said with a wry grin, "I'll have to eat this. We wouldn't want it to go to waste, now would we?"

"I don't like this one bit, Edmund Teague," Kerry snapped. "If Molly or Jess finds out what we're up to . . ." She shuddered, letting the words hang significantly between them.

"Oh, relax, won't you, Kerry? They'll never know. And look at it this way: you're doing your bit for the welfare of the military—for the country's finest young men. That's important, I'd say."

She hurled a withering look at him. "I'm thinking your own welfare is all you're concerned with! Well, then, let's be about it. What exactly do you want to take with you?"

"Here, I'll help. Most everything can be tucked into my cap, I think." Using his cap as a container, they gathered assorted cutlery and other utensils. "What'll we do about a pan? We need a cooking pan."

"Tuck it into your shoe, why don't you?" Kerry suggested with impatience.

Ignoring her sarcasm, Edmund threw on his gray surtout coat. Hiding the pan Kerry handed him beneath the loose folds of his coat, he pressed his cap to his side as Kerry fairly pushed him out the door. "Hurry *up,* Edmund! This door, quickly—not the front way."

Halfway out the door, he turned and gave her a dazzling smile. "I'm your friend for life, Kerry. I won't forget this, I promise. If you ever need a favor—*anything*—you've only to ask."

At that moment, Jess walked into the kitchen, his hands pushed into his pockets and a rather strained smile on his face. "I thought I'd see if you—"

His smile faded, to be replaced by an ominous glance at Kerry and then at the cadet. "What exactly is going on here, Kerry?"

She was frozen—and so was her tongue. Edmund, trying for a quick recovery, stammered, "Mr. Dalton, sir, we were just . . ."

"You were just *what?*" His question cracked like a whip. The cadet, looking mournfully trapped, stood unmoving as the chaplain walked purposefully toward him. Jess glanced down into the cap, then sharply at Edmund. "What in the world—"

Kerry reached out hesitantly and touched his forearm. "Jess, it's nothing, really. Edmund needed—well, that is, I'm lending him some things to use—just for tonight, you understand . . . ." Her voice trailed weakly off under the force of his angry glare.

"Teague, you've done some incredibly stupid things over the past three years—but *stealing kitchen utensils?* I believe you're surpassed yourself this time. Don't you care whether you graduate or not?" His threat was clear as he berated the miserable cadet.

Kerry, irritated with herself, angry with Edmund, and furious with Jess, cried out, "Now, just a minute, Jess. He is not stealing anything!"

The narrow glare he fastened on her when he turned from Edmund made her stammer like a guilty child. "It—it was all my idea. I—I offered to lend him these things. I insisted, I did. The cadets want a good hash, and I'm helping, that's all."

The skeptical rage that flashed in his eyes squelched her indignation. When Jess turned to the cadet, he said nothing; but his cold stare of contempt pinned the boy to the doorway.

"Kerry, no!" Edmund quickly defended her, his voice shaky but determined. "Sir, this is all my fault. I asked Kerry for help, and I—well, I forced her to lend me these things. She didn't want to do it, no, sir. I was going to return everything first thing in the morning, Mr. Dalton, really I was. Please, sir, I wouldn't steal anything."

Jess's countenance bore no hint of softening under the young man's plea. He put up a hand to silence him and then he spoke in a grim, forbidding tone. "When you take something that doesn't belong to you, Mister, the customary implication is theft, I believe."

He turned to Kerry then, regarding her with a mixture of anger and disappointment. "And you, young lady—not only were you ready to be a part of this, but you lied to me by trying to excuse him of all responsibility!"

Kerry tried to protest, but Jess silenced her with a curt, "Enough!"

His warning to Edmund was more a threat. "You do realize, of course, that I'll put you on report for this. I should have thought, Mr. Teague, that you'd have a bit more concern for your conduct record, being only a few months away from graduation. If I'm not badly mistaken, this episode might just put you over the required demerits for dismissal." The cadet remained silent, staring gloomily at the floor.

Kerry again tried to help her friend. "Jess, please don't. Please don't report him. It's not that bad, is it? All he was wanting to do was prepare some food for himself and his friends. Surely that's not deserving of . . ."

"There's a reason for every rule at this Academy, Kerry. Who decides which one is worthwhile to break? What happens to the man in the middle of a battlefield who decides to break a rule?"

When she again tried to speak, he held up a warning finger. "No—let me tell you what happens. He very likely may lose his life or cost the life of a friend."

"Oh, what a daft thing to say, comparing this to . . ."

"Go to your room!"

Recoiling from him as though he'd struck her, Kerry gasped with shock. "Jess!"

He took a quick step toward her before repeating his scalding command. "I *said* go to your room, Kerry! *Now!*"

She turned and fled, blinded by the furious tears that burned at her eyes, choking on the angry words she wanted to hurl at him.

Upstairs, she waited in her cold bedroom, unwilling to expend the energy to build a fire. Once her rage had weakened, she was overcome by guilt and anxiety, wondering when he'd come to her and what he would say.

Oh, how *could* she have been so stupid? She'd known it was wrong, that she shouldn't go along with Edmund's scheme. But she'd only wanted to help—and it hadn't seemed that bad. Instead, Edmund was now facing the possibility of being dismissed from the Academy. And that was doubly disastrous for such a man as he, coming from a family of no prestige, gaining his appointment only through the kindness of a congressman impressed by the young man's hard work and intelligence. Wherever would he go if he should have to leave? What would he do? He'd told her that West Point was his one chance to pull himself up out of the undesirable neighborhood where he'd been reared, his golden opportunity to be someone. What if she had helped destroy all that for him? An hour later, she was still huddled under an afghan, sitting on the window seat waiting to hear from Jess. Apparently he intended to make her worry a bit before facing him. And worry she did. She was so overwrought about Edmund she failed to see that what was bothering her most was the knowledge that she'd disappointed Jess.

When his heavy knock finally came, she jumped as though she'd been struck. "Jess?" she called out weakly.

"Open the door, Kerry."

Hesitantly, she walked over and opened the door. He stood there, the top of his head brushing the doorframe, with no hint of sympathy or affection in his eyes. His voice was even and cold.

"I'll make this brief." He walked past her into the room, then turned, pushing one hand into his pocket and combing his hair restlessly with the fingers of the other.

"I want to be absolutely certain that you're aware of what you've done. Not only have you been a party to a cadet's deliberate violation of the rules, but you've quite possibly aided him in getting himself dismissed from the Academy."

Holding up a hand to quiet her protest, he continued in short, clipped syllables. "Until I tell you otherwise, you'll not set foot out of this house nor entertain anyone inside it. I would advise you not to get yourself into any more trouble, young lady."

Seething at the way he was talking to her, as though she were a wee wane, Kerry pulled herself up to all the height she could manage. "You needn't be referring to me as any *lady,* Jess Dalton! We both know that I'm not—and never will be—in *your* eyes, at least."

She quickly turned from him, blinded by tears she refused to let him see. Hearing his sharp intake of breath, she half expected to feel his large hand on her arm, forcing her around to face him. But after a few seconds had passed, the bedroom door slammed shut with a loud thud, and his heavy footsteps descended the stairs.

CHAPTER TEN

Kerry suspected that Molly had overheard at least a part of the argument between her and Jess the night before, since she pointedly left them alone during breakfast the next morning.

They sat in silence at the gateleg table in the dining room. Jess always preferred to have his breakfast there so he could look out beyond the bluff. Other than a mumbled "good morning," he hadn't spoken a word to her since she entered the room.

Kerry left untouched the tasty warm fruit rolls heaped on a platter in the middle of the table; two bites of the hot ham she usually enjoyed so much had lodged in her throat so she dared not eat anything else. Miserably, she observed that Jess seemed to be unaware of her presence throughout most of the meal. He sat impassively, looking remote and formal even in his shirtsleeves, as she stared out the window at the leaden gray, gloom-misted morning.

When he slowly turned toward her, his direct gaze made her clear her throat awkwardly. But his tone, when he finally spoke, was surprisingly apologetic. "Kerry—I'm sorry I lost my temper with you last night."

Still watching her closely, he leaned back in the dark mahogany chair with its serpentine curved arms, lacing the fingers of his big hands together under his chin. Kerry continued to stare at her plate without answering, not so much from sullenness as simply not knowing what to say.

"You seemed to think I was unfair . . ."

"You had a right to be angry, I'm sure." She made her soft admission quickly, not meeting his gaze.

"Can we forget about rights for a moment? I'd like to think you understand why your actions upset me so much." He straightened and moved his chair closer to her, touching her forearm lightly.

"I may have seemed unfair to you, but I don't think you comprehend the importance of the rules for these cadets. There's a reason for all of them, believe me."

She looked at him then, finding it difficult to reconcile the gentleness brimming in his blue eyes with the harshness she'd seen there the night before. "I know it was wrong, Jess. Edmund and I were both wrong to take things from your kitchen like that. But at the time . . . well, I only meant to help him, you see. He meant no real harm. Must you place him on report?"

"Is he so important to you?" he demanded sharply, unable to deny the jealousy which ground its heel against his heart.

"And why would I not be concerned for him?" She toyed with the cuffs on the sleeves of her blouse. *Why was he so set against Edmund? It wasn't like Jess to be unfair.* "We're friends, Edmund and I. We have much in common, and we understand each other. Of course, I'm not wanting to see him fail here."

"What exactly do you have in common with Edmund Teague?" Her defense of the cadet irked him unreasonably.

Kerry could see that he was getting testy again, and she was suddenly impatient with him. It would be nice to carry on a civil conversation with him without being interrogated. If she didn't know better, she'd believe he was jealous of Edmund. That, of course, was ridiculous, only wishful thinking on her part. But why, then, was he being such a bear about all this?

"For one thing, Jess, Edmund and I come from similar backgrounds, although his family is a bit more well-off than mine, perhaps. Neither of us, however, can claim any wealth or fine breeding. Edmund did manage to get himself an education, but he still does not consider himself a gentleman any more than I think of myself as a fine lady."

He startled her by clanging his fork against his plate angrily. "When *will* you be done with this—this obsession you have about your background, Kerry? What do I have to do to make you realize it doesn't matter?"

What he actually wanted to say was that she was a wonderful girl, far lovelier and brighter and more sensitive than any lady he'd ever known. Certainly she didn't need to be casting her lot with a penniless cadet who might be interested in nothing more than taking advantage of her and tossing her aside. No, no, that was unfair. Teague wasn't that kind of fellow, and he knew it. Still, what about the stew he'd gotten her into last evening? *How would she respond,* he wondered, allowing himself to give in to a more and more frequent daydream, *if I were to tell her how very special she is to me? What would be the consequences of revealing to her that the first thing I think of when I awaken in the morning is her sunny face, and the last thing I see before I close my eyes at night is the smile in her eyes? Would she be horrified? Or, even worse, amused?*

At the moment, she appeared to be merely exasperated with him. Feeling a warning flash of her quicksilver temper, she concealed her hands in her lap, clenching them into tight fists. Her eyes glinted with hostility when she replied, "It may well be of no consequence to you, Jess, but it is to me! And Edmund Teague understands that. Perhaps that's why I wanted to help him. Certainly *you* could never comprehend what it's like to be hungry. But you may be sure that *I* do."

Her anger suddenly quenched by the unexpected outburst, she dropped her gaze to her plate and said morosely in a much lower voice, "I see now that it was wrong. But we meant no real harm, and it simply makes me ill to think that Edmund may have to leave the Academy because of such a childish mistake—especially when it was as much my fault as his." She waited tensely for the rebuke that would surely follow, fervently wishing she managed to keep her silence.

Jess surprised her by remaining quiet for what seemed an interminable time. She refused to look at him but was aware of his soft, rhythmic breathing, the light tapping of his fingertips on the table. When he finally spoke again, his tone was surprisingly mild. "I won't promise you anything right now. But—I will think about it today. I won't put the boy on report before tomorrow, seeing that he means so much to you." *She has a right to care about him—and obviously she does. Perhaps, if he's that important to her, I shouldn't be too harsh . . . it might mean his dismissal, after all. And she does need a friend her own age. . . .*

Her eyes lighted with disbelieving hopefulness. "Oh, Jess! Sure, and I couldn't be asking for more than that. It's simply not fair, now is it, that Edmund should pay so much when I was just as wrong?"

His voice took on a stern firmness again. "Now, Kerry,

I'm not *promising* anything. Don't try to anticipate me."

"No, no, I'm not," she assured him quickly, jumping up from her chair. "I understand—but I'm so grateful that you're at least willing to consider it. Here, let me get you some more hot coffee."

"That won't work, young lady. I don't want any more coffee, and you needn't turn those shamrock eyes on me. I'll do what I think should be done, so don't waste your effort on. . . ."

Her knowing smile stopped him short. Could anyone stay angry with that winsome face for long?

He shook his head in self-reproach as he stood up, mumbling in a gruff voice she suspected was somewhat of an effort to muster, "Eat your breakfast now. You've hardly touched anything."

"Oh, Jess. . . ." Did she dare remind him?

"Mm?" He turned toward her, and she caught a glimpse of the smile that had formed as he started out of the room.

"I—did you mean it last night, that I'm not to leave the house for—a while?" She bit at her lower lip anxiously, not wanting to push his patience too far.

Staring at her blankly for a moment, he finally remembered the angry command he'd issued the night before. "I—why do you ask?"

"Don't you recall? Cadet Grant was to call for me this afternoon and take me to a horsemanship demonstration at the riding stables. I thought you'd already told him I could go."

Her eyes, bright with eagerness, seemed to temper his mood further. "Yes, so I did. Well, I suppose we mustn't renege on our commitment."

He ran a hand briskly through his already tousled hair, cleared his throat, and gave her an uncertain smile. "Kerry . . . about last night. I . . . ah . . . shouldn't have spoken to you as I did. Perhaps my brusqueness comes from being around the military so much. At any rate, you are a young lady now, and I must remember to treat you accordingly."

Impulsively, he walked over to her and gave her shoulder a light squeeze. "You go along with Sam—Mr. Grant—this afternoon. And enjoy yourself."

Sure and wasn't he a good kind man? Kerry mused. Affection for him welled up in her as she watched him leave the room.

Kerry did enjoy her afternoon with Cadet Grant for a variety of reasons, not the least of which was his good-natured manner. She had met the young cadet, well-known about the Academy for his superior horsemanship, one day when she'd gone with Jess to the stables to watch Grant break a "bad" horse. His success with the most difficult animals had become almost legendary in his four years at the Point. Watching him with great interest as he worked with the high-spirited bay, Kerry had sensed the kindness and intelligence of the small, sandy-haired young man. In talking with him and Jess later, she learned what the other cadets—and most of the faculty—already knew: Except for its horses, Sam Grant would not miss the Academy when he graduated. He was not at all enamored with military life, but he loved the fine animals at his disposal.

Today, as he pointed out to Kerry some of a classmate's more sophisticated maneuvers with a handsome, sorrel gelding, she found herself wishing—as she often did—that she could once more feel the exciting power of such a fine animal beneath her. Riding had been a part of her life from the time she was a child until she'd come to America. Indeed, the times she'd felt most free and alive had been her times on horseback.

"He's a prize, isn't he?" Cadet Grant's soft voice broke into her reverie.

"Aye, he's splendid!" she exclaimed, never taking her

eyes off the beautiful animal. "I should think riding him would be like riding the wind!"

"Do you ride, Miss O'Neill?"

"Oh, yes, that is, I did in the old country."

He nodded with understanding. "Ireland is well known for its excellent horses. Did you ride in shows?"

"Oh, my, no. That's mostly for the aristocracy, you see. Nevertheless, I was fortunate enough to ride some truly grand horses. My brother was a stable hand for Lord William Trowell, a generous man. I was allowed to help exercise many of the horses on Lord William's estate."

"Ah, then you must ride quite well," he said thoughtfully.

"I could handle most of them, thanks to Liam. He tried to teach me all he knew."

"Am I correct in thinking you'd still enjoy a good ride?" he asked with a smile.

Her eyes widened at his question. "Well, of course, I would, but . . ."

"I'm sure we could arrange it for you. Would you like to take the sorrel out?" he asked, nodding toward the horse involved in the demonstration they'd been watching.

"Oh, are you certain, Mr. Grant? Would it really be all right?" She could feel her pulse accelerate with excitement.

"I don't know why not—he's a good, dependable animal. You'd enjoy him, I'm sure. Shall I get him ready?"

"But I have no habit."

He made a dismissing gesture with one hand. "You won't need one, riding sidesaddle. Wait here, I won't be long."

Sidesaddle! She'd always ridden astride back home, often bareback. Not once—never in her entire life—had she ridden sidesaddle! But if she told him that, he'd likely discard the whole idea. Of course she could do it. Hadn't her da always said she could ride anything? What could be so difficult about a sidesaddle, after all? To have a well-trained horse beneath her again, to sit the saddle of a grand animal, to feel the power and the heady freedom—not for anything would she miss this opportunity.

Within a few moments, Cadet Grant was back for her. With a pleased grin, he guided her toward the entrance to the barn where the proud, well-muscled horse was saddled and waiting. "Oh, isn't he grand!" Kerry exclaimed as they approached. She could hardly wait to climb up on him.

"His name is Freedom," the cadet informed her. "As a matter of fact, he's a gift to the Academy from Mr. Dalton. By the way, I've given him orders to be on his best behavior."

With a skeptical eye, Kerry studied the odd-looking saddle on the horse. *It won't be all that difficult,* she told herself firmly. *All I have to do is climb on—and hold on. It's still no more than a horse and a saddle, after all.*

Gathering the reins in her hands, she climbed up as smoothly as possible, tucking her left foot into the single stirrup as she leaned her right knee slightly against the knobby protuberance at the front of the saddle. Accustomed to using her legs to signal the horse when she rode astride, she couldn't for the life of her figure out how to give signals when she couldn't mold her legs to the horse. Finally, with what she hoped was a safe gesture, she nudged him gently with her stirruped left foot.

The sorrel picked up the signal instantly, raising ever so slightly his front feet from the ground and bounding off into the woods. Pulling back lightly on the reins, Kerry slowed him to an easy, ground-covering canter. His gait was as smooth as an old rocking horse, and it took her no time to get her seat and enjoy her ride. Freedom was soon responding to her as though they were longtime friends.

Ah, how I have missed this, she thought to herself, exulting in the feel of the cold wind whipping her face and the comforting motion of the animal beneath her. *Wouldn't it be grand if Jess and I could ride together. . . .*

"Sure and you're a splendid thing, Freedom," she

murmured to the horse, smiling at the name Jess had given him. "Cadet Grant said you were a gift to the academy from Jess. I'm thinking you're a very special gift to me, too."

Approaching the stable to seek out Grant and Kerry, Jess spied the cadet talking with one of the grooms just outside. "Has Kerry—Miss O'Neill—gone back to the house already?"

"Oh, no, sir, Mr. Dalton. She's off for a ride with Freedom. She certainly sits a horse well, doesn't she, sir?"

The unknowing young cadet was totally unprepared for the violent reaction of the chaplain towering over him. The anger that darkened Jess's features was a direct contrast to the glow of happiness Sam had seen on Kerry's face as she rode off only moments before.

"*You put her on a horse?*" Jess demanded incredulously.

"Why—yes, sir," Grant replied uncertainly. "Is something wrong, sir?"

"You allowed her to go out riding alone? Where did she go?" Jess felt a rising wave of nausea assault his senses.

"I—Mr. Dalton, sir, she's only been gone a few minutes. What is it, sir—what's wrong?" The rage in Jess's eyes made the bewildered cadet retreat as though he'd been struck.

"Get me a horse saddled, Grant—now!" *You wouldn't let it happen again, would You, Lord. Please, God . . . it couldn't happen again, could it? It's not like it was with Emily. . . .*

"Yes, sir, of course—" Grant stammered. "But, sir, she's an excellent rider. She said she's ridden since she was a child. I could tell she's quite comfortable on—"

"What kind of saddle did you put her on?" Jess snapped out his words like rifle shots.

"Saddle, sir? Why—side, of course."

"Grant—she's an Irish farm girl," Jess said, his voice deceptively quiet. "I doubt she's even seen a sidesaddle except in a horse show."

103

Understanding dawned in the cadet's eyes, and he raised a shaky hand to his forehead. "But she didn't say a word."

"No, I'm sure she didn't. She'd be too stubborn, no doubt." Jess's expression had returned to a thunderous mask.

The sensitive cadet, however, realized with astonishment that another emotion was behind the chaplain's uncharacteristic behavior. Mr. Dalton was frightened. This man, who represented a rock of strength to almost every cadet at the Academy, was obviously shaken, and Grant felt his own stirrings of alarm.

He attempted to reassure Jess. "Still, sir, she was doing just fine. I watched her until she was out of my view. But I'll saddle York and go for her myself if you think . . . ."

Both men whirled around at the sound of approaching hoofbeats. Kerry, her face radiantly flushed as much from a deep glow of happiness as from the brisk, cold air, didn't notice the storm brewing in Jess's eyes.

She brought the horse to an abrupt stop a few feet from the men, glancing from one to the other with excited pleasure. "Oh, Jess, I wish you'd been with me!" she exclaimed with delight. "Mr. Grant said he was a prize, and truly he is."

Jess was beside her before she knew what was happening. A startled protest escaped her when he reached up and roughly pulled her from the saddle. Grant quickly took the reins, practically leading the horse right out from under her. "What—*Jess!* Whatever are you doing?"

"Don't you ever do that again!" he lashed out at her, his eyes scalding her with the heat of his fury as he set her rudely onto her feet.

Dumbfounded and totally in the dark as to why he was raving at her like a madman, Kerry shrieked at him. "Don't do *what* again?" He had his enormous hands locked about her waist in a death grip, and he looked to be no more than a beat away from a seizure! "Will you stop crushing me, for goodness' sake?

Bile rose in his throat as the full weight of his fear settled over him. He moved his hands from about her waist and roughly grasped her shoulders, stopping just short of shaking her. "What were you thinking of, going off like that alone?" he yelled at her, his eyes still blazing fire. "Don't you have any consideration at all for anyone besides yourself?"

Kerry gasped in amazement, pushing her hands against his chest with all the force she could muster, trying to free herself from his hold on her. "Are you *daft*, Jess Dalton? You're acting like a man possessed. Let me go—do you hear me, let me go this instant!"

The unexpected strength of her shove against him caught Jess off guard, and he dropped his hands. He suddenly realized the small, shocked face glaring up at him was sincerely bewildered. She hadn't a glimmer of an idea why he was so distraught. How could she? She didn't know about Emily; she didn't know about the accident—and she didn't know how very dear she was to him.

Kerry watched him with astonishment, as the anger ebbed and finally faded from his eyes. Another emotion slowly settled in its place, but she was too frustrated and befuddled to try and discern the change in him. How dare he treat her like this! Oh, the man was such a riddle! Only this morning he'd apologized for being so hard on her the night before. Now he was at it again—only this time she didn't even know what she'd done. Would he never stop driving her out of her wits with his erratic behavior?

Still, something nagged at the back of her mind, some vague awareness she couldn't quite bring into focus. Her mind groped to clarify whatever was teasing at her memory, and at last she recalled what Molly had told her about the woman Jess had once loved, his Miss Emily. Of course! Hadn't she died in a riding accident? A wild idea began to skate through her mind. Was it possible that Jess had been afraid for her, afraid that the same thing might happen to her that had happened to his former fiancée? No, that was ridiculous.

"Kerry—I'm sorry. . . ." His voice was soft but ragged as he wiped an unsteady hand over his eyes, avoiding her gaze. "I didn't mean to shout at you like that—but you frightened me so terribly."

She stared at him with disbelief. He'd been frightened for her? Worried about her? The uncertain, apologetic look he turned on her tugged at her heart. Instinctively, she moved closer to him, reaching out with one hand to touch his forearm. "Jess—I never once thought you'd worry about me."

His voice was thick with emotion and far less confident than usual when he replied. "You did—give me a fright, dear." Almost shyly, he touched the hand she'd placed on his arm, then enfolded it gently within his own. Giving her a sheepish smile, he drew her closer, resting his chin lightly on the top of her head for a moment. "I didn't even know whether you could ride, especially sidesaddle."

"Oh, I can't—I mean I couldn't!"

"What?" He moved back to look at her.

"Ride a sidesaddle." She grinned mischievously at him, her eyes dancing with fun. "But I can now."

"Kerry," he groaned, shaking his head back and forth in wonder. "What am I to do with you?"

"Were you really that concerned about me?" she asked quietly.

Looking down at her upturned face, he felt his throat constrict and he longed to crushed her to him. "Do you need to ask—after seeing the fool I made of myself?" he muttered.

"You weren't a bit foolish, Jess," she told him, her voice catching on a note of huskiness. "But it's nice that you care so much. And I won't go out alone again if it makes you fret."

He sighed with relief. With his arm about her shoulders, he moved her toward the path leading away from the riding stables. "We'd best be getting home. Molly will be in a state by now." He hugged her to his side for an instant before walking on.

Neither of them even noticed Sam Grant leaning against the outside wall of the stable, chewing idly on a piece of straw and watching them with a pleased smile as they walked away.

CHAPTER ELEVEN

Late the next afternoon, as the day grew darker with a threatening snowstorm, Kerry tied the finishing knot in an embroidered mirror frame she was doing for Molly's Christmas gift. The housekeeper had taken an unusual break in her busy routine, and Kerry quickly took advantage of it. Once the frame was completed, she tucked it into a pillowcase and hid it in the blanket chest in her room.

Somewhat concerned about Molly's strange behavior, she went to check on her, knocking lightly at the door down the hall from her own bedroom. When there was no reply, she peeked in and was surprised to see Molly bundled into bed under a heap of quilts, looking flushed and ill.

"Why, Molly, whatever is the matter?" She hurried over to the bedside, receiving an impatient scowl when she placed her hand on the older woman's forehead.

"Don't now, I fear it's the grippe. You must stay out of

here, for what is our Jess to do if both of us should be abed?"

Kerry could sense the great effort behind Molly's command. "I'll do no such thing, and you needn't be wasting your breath. Simply tell me what I should do to help you."

"If you don't want our Jess turning you across his knee when I tell him you've been acting like a spoiled tad again, you'd best be getting yourself from this room, Miss—at once, d'you hear me?"

The uncharacteristic weakness in Molly's voice alarmed Kerry, but she knew better than to show it. Planting her hands determinedly on her hips, she glared fiercely at the housekeeper. "Tell him whatever you like, Molly Larkin, but no man will take his hand to *this* lass, I can promise you that! Since you're so eager to be handing out advice, will you not offer some that makes a bit more sense?"

Kerry knew Molly was extremely ill when the feisty older woman made no effort to challenge her. Placing her hand against Molly's cheek, she winced as she felt heat sear her own skin. Sure, and Molly's fever must be dangerously high.

Saying no more, she hurried from the room and ran downstairs. Throwing on her cape, she rushed out the kitchen door. A light, frosty snow had begun, and the wind pelted it relentlessly against her face as she dashed across the grounds to the Plain. The main parade ground was almost deserted at this hour; most of the cadets were attending their recitations in the Academic Building.

Racing into the building which housed the classrooms, she breathlessly approached the first cadet she spied. "Please, sir—could you help me find the chaplain, Mr. Dalton?"

The tall, blond upperclassman smiled down at the petite young lady clutching his arm, her cheeks crimson from the cold, her long eyelashes iced with traces of freezing snow. But his pleased expression rapidly disappeared when he saw the alarm in her eyes.

"It's Molly Larkin, you see. She's terribly ill, and I need Jess—Mr. Dalton—to come home right away."

"I believe he's just down the hall, miss, in his philosophy class. Come on, I'll take you to him."

Coming to an abrupt halt in front of the closed door of a large classroom, the cadet rapped sharply to draw Jess's attention.

"Kerry!" he exclaimed, frowning in surprised concern when he stepped out into the hall. "What are you doing here?"

"Oh, Jess, can you come home? It's Molly—I think she's terribly ill. She says it's the grippe, and her fever is *that* high! I left her alone to come for you, but I fear she shouldn't be by herself."

"Hampton—finish up for me here, would you, then dismiss the class," he instructed the cadet standing by Kerry. Not waiting for a reply, he grabbed his greatcoat from a hook, tucked Kerry's arm snugly inside the crook of his elbow, and walked swiftly down the hallway.

Half-running the distance to the house, they steamed the air with their labored breathing in the frigid, snow-laced wind. "I can't recall Molly's ever being ill before," Jess told her. "I should never have let her visit the Superintendent's wife the other night."

"She wouldn't have listened, even if you'd tried to stop her—you know how she is," Kerry gasped into the biting air, her feet skimming the ground as he practically carried her along beside him. With her free hand she attempted to pull her hood tighter about her face.

Once inside the house, Jess tossed his coat onto a chair and took the stairs two at a time, with Kerry right behind him. Flanking Molly on either side of the bed, their worried gazes met when she let out a low moan.

"Whatever are you doing home at this time of the day, Jess?" Her usually strong, impatient voice was little more than a raspy whisper, and her face was crimson with the flush of fever.

"I though Kerry might need a bit of help keeping you in bed," he told her dryly. With one hand on her forehead and the other gently holding her wrist, he frowned when he felt the heat of her skin.

"Kerry," he said softly without looking at her, "I want you to stay out of here."

"I'll not," she declared firmly, shrugging out of her cape and throwing it over Molly's rocking chair. "I've already been exposed to whatever it is, so I'll be staying. Just tell me what to do for her."

His concern was evident in his glance across the bed. "All right—but keep your distance. Get a cool cloth for her head. I'm going to find Dr. Greene."

Within moments, the doctor confirmed their fears that Molly was indeed the victim of influenza. For several hours after Dr. Greene left, Kerry stayed by Molly's bed refusing to leave even when Jess threatened to carry her from the room. She faithfully applied cool wrappings to the older woman's head, often moistening her lips with lemon ice.

Finally, when Molly seemed to be resting somewhat easier, she allowed Jess to coax her out long enough to get something to eat. "I'll stay with her, Kerry—you go down to the kitchen and have some supper."

She went reluctantly, but found herself unable to eat. After only a few sips of tea, she fixed a cup for Jess and went back upstairs.

Both of them spent the next few hours beside Molly, Jess in a straight-backed chair on one side of the bed, Kerry in the rocker on the other side, where she eventually fell into an uneasy sleep.

112

As he studied her small form curled in the large chair, Jess thought she looked extremely young and vulnerable—as well as uncomfortable. Touching Molly lightly to be sure her fever was no higher, he went around to Kerry, tugged gently at her shoulder and pulled her to her feet.

"Come on, dear," he whispered into the soft fragrance of her tousled hair, "you're exhausted. I want you to go to bed now."

"No," she mumbled, not quite awake. "I'm staying with Molly."

"No, you're not," he told her firmly. "I need you wide-awake tomorrow to look after her so I can take my classes. Come along now." With his arm around her, he led her across the room and out the door, smiling as he moved her along to her bedroom door, where he stopped. Bracing his arm on the doorframe in the dimly lighted hall, he looked down into her sleepy eyes with a thoughtful smile.

"You truly care about Molly, don't you?"

She looked up at him with surprise. "Of course I do. Molly is . . . well, I suppose I feel toward her much as I would have toward my own mother, had I known her," she admitted candidly. "Yes, Molly is important to me."

"That would please her no end, Kerry. She loves you, you know."

She stared at him blankly, still dazed with fatigue and the remaining traces of her fitful nap. "Molly? Loves *me?*"

He nodded. "Indeed she does. I've known her for a long time, and there's no mistaking her feelings for you."

"But—she's always fussing at me."

He smiled with understanding, reaching out to tuck a stubborn curl behind her ear. "Yes, I know. But that's just her way. She's not a woman to wear her heart on her sleeve. But you can take my word for it—you're very dear to her."

"Well, I suppose I'll have to remember that the next time

113

she comes flying at me in a state. I'll simply remind myself how much she loves me."

"People have different ways of showing their love, Kerry," Jess replied in answer to her skepticism. "Molly often shows hers rather . . . fiercely."

Perhaps if she'd been fully awake and less exhausted, she would never have been so bold. But the soft, flickering glow of the candle in the wall sconce, the close, intimate atmosphere, and the warmth brimming in his gaze betrayed her senses by weaving a filmy web of fantasy around the moment. "And you, Jess?" she murmured. "How would you be showing it, if you loved someone?" As soon as the words tumbled out, she caught her lower lip between her teeth, appalled at what she'd just said.

But he simply smiled a sweet, wonderful smile, his gaze lingering over her drowsy features as though he would engrave her upon his memory. His eyes reflected the candlelight as he studied her, and the glow Kerry saw there mirrored her own depth of feeling.

She stood motionless as Jess lowered his face to hers with a slow, dreamlike movement, until his lips were no more than a soft breath away, warming her lips with a sweet whisper. "Ah, Kerry . . . I'm afraid you already know the answer to that. . . ."

His dark eyelashes brushed her cheek as he touched his lips to hers with a kiss as soft and tender as a spring night's breeze. When he lifted his face from hers, his features still softened by a smile, Kerry tipped her head to rest against the warmth of his shoulder for an instant, feeling his lips press tenderly against the top of her head. Finally, with a deep sigh, he put her carefully away from him, turning her gently around toward her open bedroom door. "Get some sleep now, dear," he urged in a broken whisper.

CHAPTER TWELVE

Kerry and Jess took turns caring for Molly during the next three days. He still had his daily teaching and chaplain's duties to attend to, but he spelled Kerry as much as he could, especially at night.

On Thursday evening, Kerry met him at the door with the good news that Molly was finally showing some improvement. Smiling with relief, he pounded the snow from his boots and brushed it off his coat. Then taking Kerry's arm, he started upstairs toward Molly's room.

"We're in for quite a storm, I fear; the snow is already heavy. So, what did Dr. Greene have to say this afternoon?"

"He thinks we'll see a big improvement by morning. We're to make certain she takes lots of juices and some soup. I made some chicken broth earlier."

Molly was in a sound sleep when they looked in on her so they quietly left the room and went downstairs to the kitchen. Kerry watched Jess lift each lid from the variety of pans on the stove to inspect the contents.

"Molly's taught me well enough how you like your food," she snapped at him. "You won't be starving while she's ill."

He looked at her blankly for a moment, then grinned contritely. "I wasn't worried—only curious."

He showered her with praise throughout the meal to show his confidence in her. "I'm impressed," he said over a plate filled with smoked ham and creamed potatoes. "This is every bit as good as Molly's." He ate with relish, protesting when Kerry scooped up a second helping for him, although he didn't refuse it.

Finishing the last bite of his dessert, a generous piece of pumpkin pie, he declared he wouldn't eat for the rest of the week. "We are definitely going for a walk tonight—a very long walk," he announced, pushing himself back from the table with a great display of effort.

"Oh, but it's too cold." Kerry shivered at the thought, hearing the wind slice wickedly through the grove of pine trees behind the house.

His eyes glinted with amusement. "I should warn you, I suppose, that this is actually rather mild for West Point."

Giving him a skeptical look, she left him to finish his coffee while she took some broth to Molly. She was able to coax only a few sips into the housekeeper, but felt pleased for that. When Molly dropped her head back with a weak smile, obviously exhausted from her slight effort, Kerry plumped her pillows for her and smoothed the bed linens.

"I feel such a fool lying abed while you do all the work and care for Jess," she protested in a weary voice.

"We're getting on just fine, so you needn't be bothering yourself now. Why, Jess even paid me a compliment or two on my cooking tonight. What d'you think of that?"

But Molly's eyes were already half-closed. By the time

Kerry straightened her bedding and stirred up the fire she was sound asleep again.

When she returned to the kitchen, she found Jess stacking their dinner dishes in the sink. "Is Molly all right?" he asked, turning toward her.

"She's sleeping again. Whatever are you doing, Jess? Molly would crack both our heads if she found out you'd turned a hand in the kitchen."

He lifted one dark brow in amusement. "And wouldn't she be amazed to find out I didn't so much as drop a dish? All right, Kerry Shannon—get your boots on. We're going for a walk in the snow."

With a pleased smile, Kerry fetched her new leather boots from the hall closet, quickly snuggling her small feet into them. These were her most cherished possession, not so much because of their excellent quality, though they were skillfully made, but more because Jess had had them made just for her and shipped upriver from New York City.

Laughing like children, they plunged into the enormous drifts of snow in back of the house. When Kerry lifted her face to catch a few heavy flakes with her mouth, she lost her balance and very nearly tumbled into a large pile of snow. Jess steadied her, chuckling at her surprised expression as he removed his well-worn gray muffler and wrapped it securely around her throat. "There. That should keep Jack Frost from biting at you."

"I wouldn't be feeling it if he did," she yelled into the wind. "I'm numb."

"I can see I'm going to have to toughen you up, young lady. You'll never make it through a West Point winter otherwise." The words were no more out of his mouth than he scooped up a handful of snow and sent it sailing toward her.

Kerry quickly raised an arm to shield her face, and the snowball exploded against her hand. "You'll be paying for that, Jess Dalton," she whooped, hurling a snowball of her own at him.

Her aim was far better than he'd expected; the snow caught him full in the face, spraying into his beard. Kerry doubled over with laughter and waved a taunting hand at him. "You look like a frozen grizzly bear, Mr. Dalton, sir."

"Oh, do I now?" he challenged, stopping to brush the snow away from his nose. "You know, don't you, that grizzly bears are mean tempered and attack when they're provoked?" With a loud, convincing roar, he charged at her, holding another snowball ready. "You think you're cold now? Just wait."

"No, Jess—you wouldn't! No, please!" she howled, trying to turn and run. But her feet went out from under her on a patch of ice, sending her sprawling into a most unladylike position.

"Ohhh. I'm all wet. I'm freezing!"

Kerry thought his frown of concern looked suspicious as he knelt down beside her. "Come on, let's get you inside before you catch cold." Effortlessly, he scooped her up into his arms and began to trudge slowly through the snow toward the back porch. "I certainly don't want two slugabeds on my hands. There's only so much a man can tolerate, you know," he teased, smiling down at her.

Locking her hands around his neck, Kerry studied him. Her mind suddenly reeled with confusion when she met his gaze and saw a tenderness warm enough to melt all the snow around them. He stumbled slightly, but his eyes never left her face. "Do you know, Kerry Shannon, that you have springtime in your eyes?" His voice was thick and unsteady. "Springtime and emeralds and faraway places. . . ."

When he dipped his head down to lightly touch his lips to her forehead, the only reply Kerry trusted herself with was a shy, happy smile as she tightened her arms about his neck.

Once inside, he loosened her cape and unbundled her as he would have a child, setting her down on the long plank bench in the hallway while he knelt to remove her boots. He rubbed her chilled feet between his hands, smiling at their daintiness.

"You have feet like one of those elegant little china dolls," he said. Her innocent, childlike sweetness could easily melt his heart, he marveled, while her delicate loveliness assailed his emotions in an entirely different way.

"And they've just as l-little f-feeling, too," she croaked, shivering from head to toe. "I told you this was no night to be outdoors."

Ignoring her complaints, he rose and tossed his wet coat over the bench beside her. "Stay right here, I'll only be a moment."

He returned with a large towel and immediately began to rub her hair dry, meeting her glare with a wry grin.

"That's better, curly-top," he told her, giving one still-damp lock of hair a gentle tug. "Now, go upstairs and put on a dry dress while I build a fire in the study. And look in on Molly while you're up there, would you?"

Fussing at him over her shoulder, she raced up the stairs and changed into one of the new dresses Molly had made for her, a soft wool in a shade of dusty rose. The flush on her cheeks—painted by the cold night air and the happiness she'd been feeling all evening—almost matched perfectly the color of the dress.

She found Molly still sleeping peacefully. Touching her lightly on the cheek to make sure the fever hadn't returned, she tucked the covers more snugly about her shoulders and quietly tiptoed from the room.

Downstairs, Jess had a cheerful fire blazing in the study fireplace and stood facing it, his hands outstretched to warm them. Kerry stopped for a moment, feeling a wave of affection for him well up deep within her as she studied him. In his blue-and-gray flannel shirt, his skin wind-whipped with color, she thought he looked wonderfully handsome and fit.

He turned toward her as she entered the study, his eyes scanning her with appreciation. "Amazing," he murmured.

"What?"

"That you can wear that color—and wear it so well. It should be abominable with your red hair."

"My hair is not red," she retorted.

"Of course, it isn't," he agreed blandly, grinning at the spark flaring in her eyes. "Here, put this around you," he ordered, draping a soft white afghan around her shoulders and gently moving her toward the settee.

"I've been meaning to tell you," he said offhandedly as she sat down. "but with all the confusion of Molly's illness, it slipped my mind. I decided not to put Cadet Teague on report . . . this time."

"Oh, Jess, how kind of you!" she exclaimed, looking up at him with a pleased expression.

"Well, he knows he's going to have to be on his very best behavior from now until graduation—or else," he muttered gruffly.

Walking over to the bookshelves, he selected a volume bound in rich, coffee-colored leather. "I think you might enjoy this," he said, returning to her and placing the book in her hands.

She looked at it curiously. *"Oliver Twist.* Have you read it, Jess?"

He nodded. "Mr. Dickens is a great champion of the poor. He's fighting his own war against poverty and abuse, but he uses his pen rather than a gun."

Her eyes crinkled as she smiled at him. "Like you. You're a part of that war as well, Jess."

"I used to think I was," he said ruefully. "But lately I find myself wondering if perhaps the battle was lost before I ever got into it." Walking over to the window, he drew one side of the draperies back and looked out at the heavy, sweeping snow blowing against the porch.

Finally he turned, straightened his shoulders, and came to sit next to Kerry on the settee. He leaned back, settling himself with his hands laced behind his head. "Why don't you read to me?"

"Aloud, d'you mean?"

"Please," he replied, closing his eyes with a contented smile. "I love the lilt in your voice, do you know that? I can be exhausted or out of sorts, but as soon as I hear your voice I feel better. You have a rhythm to your words that soothes my spirit."

She flushed with pleasure, surprised at his rare candor. Reading by the soft glow of a large candle, she quickly became a part of the world of Oliver Twist, so enthralled with the story she forgot her surroundings until she felt a light touch on her shoulder.

Glancing over, she skipped a beat in her reading when she saw that Jess had fallen asleep with his head nodding against her. A sympathetic wave of tenderness flowed over her as she watched him, noting how the fatigue and strain of the past few days had left their mark, making him appear older and so terribly tired. She longed to smooth the lock of black hair falling over his forehead and erase the weary lines fanning out from his eyes.

Basking in the sweetness of being close to him, she soon gave up reading. She placed the book beside her and moved so that she could place her arm about his broad shoulders to position him more comfortably against her. When she hesitantly laid her cheek against the top of his head for an instant, she felt a thrill of surprise at the softness of his hair against her skin. The unruly waves of sable hair that looked so crisp and springy actually had the texture of silk.

Her eyes misted with drowsy contentment as she sat, unmoving, while he leaned peacefully against her, the steady rhythm of his soft breathing lulling her to a tranquil daze. Almost asleep, she gave a small jerk of her shoulder when she felt him shift his weight slightly. Her heart seemed to leap to her throat when his arm encircled her waist and pulled her closer to him, then tightened to an embrace. The only light in the room was the flickering candle and the faint glow from the dying fire, but she could see his eyes, soft and heavy with sleep as he studied her.

"I'm sorry," he whispered. "I didn't mean to fall asleep." But he made no move to release her. Smiling, Kerry allowed her fingers to rake gently through his hair. His closeness was euphoric, soothing her to a state where everything was suspended for that moment. The arm around her waist moved her even closer to him as his other hand gently coaxed her face to his. Afraid to breathe for fear she'd lose the moment, Kerry closed her eyes—waiting.

"Kerry . . . sweet . . ." The first heady sensation of his gentle, seeking kiss surged into a tide of new, almost frightening emotions. But when he gathered her more snugly into the sanctuary of his arms, she gave herself over to the wonderful closeness she'd longed for ever since he had first kissed her weeks ago.

"Ah, Kerry . . . dear, I know I shouldn't. . . ."

She wrapped her arms around his neck to stop his words. Her heart sang at his soft, murmuring endearments and the way his eyes were adoring her. When she felt the trembling in his large hands, she thought she would surely explode with love for him. For love it was, and she knew it now. This man was the only man who would ever touch her, she promised herself at that moment, the only man she would ever belong to. In truth, her heart had been his for some time now.

An aching sadness wound its way through her when his lips brushed her cheek, then her temple, as he gently brought an end to the embrace. His breath was uneven against her hair and his broken whisper reluctant. "Kerry, I think . . . you'd best go upstairs."

She nodded, threatening his attempt to regain his composure when she turned her love-filled eyes on him. "Jess—"

"Shh, now . . ." he murmured, silencing her by gently touching his fingers to her lips. "If it were possible, I'd keep you right here, like this, forever. But I'm supposed to be taking care of you, not taking advantage of you."

She shook her head slightly, her eyes pleading with him. "Please don't say that—as though you're sorry. Don't be sorry, Jess."

Wrapping a copper tendril of her hair about his fingers, he studied her face closely. The heaviness around his heart was revealed in the despair that clouded his gaze. "No, I'm not sorry, dear . . . never sorry, to be so close to you. But—"

"What, Jess?" she prompted, hoping, hoping. . . .

"I wish . . . there weren't so many years between us, that I had a right to feel—what I'm afraid I'm feeling."

"And what are you feeling, Jess?" she whispered, half-eager, half afraid to hear his answer.

A depth of love that terrifies me, little one . . . a love unlike anything I ever thought myself capable of. . . . He avoided her gaze as he slowly eased himself away from her. "Kerry, if you were older—or if I weren't your guardian . . . ." The words hung suspended between them.

He touched her just once more, brushing his knuckles lightly across the softness of her cheek, then rose from the settee and pulled her to her feet. She saw him swallow with difficulty as he stared down at her, searching her eyes with tender longing and a helplessness that made her ache

123

to hold him, to comfort him, and reassure him. But unwilling to face another scene of rejection, she simply turned and walked out of the room as he stood and watched her with an anguished sinking of his heart.

Throughout the night she prayed, appealing to God to remove the barrier Jess had seemingly erected between the two of them. *Oh, Lord, it's as though he's built a wall around his heart. Once in awhile, he allows me to loosen a brick, but then he just replaces it with an even larger one. I do love him so, Lord . . . even though my mind tells me it's hopeless, my heart insists that it isn't. Father, he's so lonely, isn't he? And sometimes he seems so very sad. I want to end all that for him, Lord . . . . I want to put a smile in his eyes that will never go away . . . . Oh, I know I'm not the woman he deserves . . . but still, he does seem happy when he's with me, at least most of the time, now doesn't he? And surely I could learn to be all he needs, couldn't I? Certainly I'd try, Lord—You know how hard I'd try. . . .*

She finally surrendered to a fitful sleep, unaware that beneath her window, Jess roamed the yard, bundled in his black greatcoat, like a large, dark shadow crossing the white-covered ground. Indifferent to the freezing wind and snow pummeling his bowed head, he, too, prayed, seeking balm for his own misery, attempting to still the emotional tempest raging within him as furiously as the winter storm raging about him.

CHAPTER THIRTEEN

Two days before Christmas, Jess abruptly left the Point, leaving an anxious Kerry behind. It wasn't at all like him to go away with so little apparent forethought. He had explained nothing, saying only that he would be in New York City for a day or so. ·

Kerry couldn't help worrying, hoping his sudden departure had nothing to do with her or the new closeness developing between them since that night in his study when he'd revealed such an unexpected depth of emotion. Kerry had half-expected him to withdraw from her after that, but he hadn't. In fact, she'd detected a subtle change in his manner toward her; little by little he began to show his affection more freely. There was an awareness of something different now each time they were together.

Trying not to allow herself too much hope, she repeatedly told herself that nothing had actually changed. He was still obsessed with his duty and responsibility as her guardian, and she was still an Irish upstart with not a single quality a man like Jess would expect and desire in a woman.

But more and more often the tantalizing question would dart in and out of her thoughts—*How could he kiss me and hold me so tenderly, so lovingly, if he didn't care?* Jess was not a man to toy with anyone's emotions, she knew. And whatever the extent of his feelings toward her might be, she didn't doubt for a moment the sincerity of his concern. He cared too much to deliberately hurt her. What, then, was happening between them?

When she quizzed Molly on his whereabouts the afternoon before Christmas Day, she learned nothing. "Ach, and how would I be knowing what he's up to? Sure, and it's not my place to be questioning him, now is it? He simply said he would be away overnight, and off he went on the steamer."

"Is there anything wrong, d'you think?" She tried to keep the uneasiness out of her voice, but Molly's mind was too quick.

Interrupting her brisk dusting, she darted a curious glance at Kerry. "If you're looking for something to fuss about, I can think of a few more likely things than our Jess leaving for a day or so. I'd be pleased if you'd spend a bit of your attention on this parlor."

She looked sternly down her nose, resting one hand on an ample hip while the other hand hoisted the duster like a weapon. "You've done a fair job with trimming the candles and hanging the wreaths and all, but I'm thinking all these fancy decorations would be far more impressive if they were free of dust and cobwebs."

Fuming with annoyance, Kerry took a long, deep breath, reminding herself that Molly was still a bit snappish after her illness. She set about polishing the tall round lamp stand with the carved deer ornament inside the pedestal, humming softly to herself, ignoring Molly's ire.

Glancing about the room, she thought it looked quite nice—cozy and charming and "Christmasy," with evergreen wreaths hung in each window, and white candles in brass holders lining the wide front windowsill. Molly had framed the brick fireplace with a garland she'd made of laurel and gingerbread cookies.

Her favorite holiday decoration, however, was the hand-carved nativity scene which sat on the mantel among spruce branches and holly. She'd learned from Molly that Jess's grandfather had been a talented whittler and had created the set for his son, Jess's father, when he was still a small boy. Kerry loved the perfect little figures, fashioned with such obvious patience and loving care.

Her thoughts turned to the special gift she'd made for Jess. Molly had given her a precious store of soft blue yarn—the exact color of Jess's eyes, she thought with a smile—and she'd knitted a lovely muffler to replace his old gray one. He had a tendency to develop a touch of hoarseness, probably from all his walking back and forth in the cold and having to use his voice so much each day. *My gift will help to protect that fine voice,* Kerry thought proudly, *so he can continue to teach and preach to the cadets—or, as Jess would put it, to "work with my men."*

A noisy commotion in the hall snapped her abruptly out of her reverie. "Whatever is happening out there?" Molly demanded of no one in particular.

Kerry followed her through the doorway, stopping short when she saw Jess standing just past the threshold, knocking the snow from his shoes. Her heart turned a delighted flip when his eyes sought hers, locking for an instant. Watching the two of them closely, Molly lifted a speculative eyebrow, greeted him, and then returned quietly to the parlor.

Suddenly shy, Kerry could think of nothing to say. But

her eyes danced with happiness when he gave her a teasing smile over his shoulder as he hung his greatcoat on a wall hook.

"Miss me?" he asked softly.

Her words tumbled out before she could help herself. "Oh, I did, yes. Are you all right, then?"

He walked over to her, a puzzled frown lining his forehead. "Why wouldn't I be?" Tilting her chin upward with a gentle nudge of his finger, he studied her face. "What about you and Molly? Is everything all right here?"

"Of course, it is—we're fine—but—"

"But what?"

She shrugged, hoping to appear indifferent. "I might have worried a bit is all."

He placed his large hands lightly upon her narrow shoulders, studying her with a thoughtful smile. "Well, now, this is a new experience for me—being missed when I'm away. I believe I like it." The direct intensity of his gaze made her feel wobbly-kneed.

Jess's voice held a trace of amusement. "Since you're too polite to ask, I've been in New York doing some Christmas shopping. Oh, and by the way, that trunk of your father's that you couldn't bring with you? It's down at the dock. One of the cadets is going to bring it up on the wagon later." He gently smoothed back a stubborn copper curl which insisted on escaping from her hair ribbon.

Surprised and pleased, she exclaimed, "Da's trunk? But however did you get it here from Buffalo?"

"I had it shipped and stored at a warehouse in New York. Sam Grant made the arrangements for me."

With one arm around her shoulders, he moved her toward the kitchen. "I've been thinking about Molly's Christmas Eve ham all the way here—I haven't had a decent meal in two days."

"Oh, and wait until you see it—it's *that* huge!"

Dinner that evening was a merry occasion. It *was* Christmas Eve, of course, but Kerry's radiant happiness at Jess's return added to the festive mood. Her high spirits infected Jess and Molly as well.

Her exhilaration built by the hour, and trudging through the snow on their way to the chapel later that night, she was far too excited to notice the rapidly dropping temperature. This year, instead of the traditional Christmas morning sermon, Jess had decided to provide a Christmas Eve worship service for those cadets remaining at the Academy during the holidays.

He tucked Kerry's arm a little more snugly to his side as the three of them walked along, enjoying her attempts at guessing the special gift he'd hinted at earlier in the evening.

"If you're a very good girl, perhaps I will let you open *one* of your gifts tonight—a special one. But do you really think you can sit still in church and pay attention?"

Kerry, knowing that Jess was enjoying himself immensely, matched his banter. "Perhaps—if the sermon isn't too boring."

Indulging herself with the pleasure of studying him as they walked, she experienced a delicious ripple of joy. Her gaze traveled down from the black satin sheen of his curling hair, across the broad expanse of his heavy shoulders, over the long, tightly muscled length of his body. Even the heavy black greatcoat he wore couldn't disguise the obvious power of the man.

He's a giant, she thought with an audible sigh. *The biggest man I've ever known—in size, and at heart.* She colored and looked quickly away when he glanced down at her and caught her appraising him with such obvious admiration. And when he gave her a quick, impulsive hug, she didn't dare to look up at him for fear he'd see the intensity of her feelings. She allowed herself the luxury of pretending, at least for a few moments, that they were a real family on their way to church—a loving husband and wife, with their good friend, Molly.

It was a touching, beautiful worship service. The hushed chapel was fragrant with evergreen boughs, aglow with flickering candlelight. When Jess read the beloved Christmas story from the Gospel of Luke in his rich, smooth voice, it seemed to Kerry that she could almost hear the ethereal angel voices echoing throughout the peaceful stillness of the chapel. And when the cadet choir sang the haunting "O Come, O Come, Emmanuel," its unaccompanied strains weaving in and out between the large columns, her heart soared, exulting in the meaning and beauty of this special night.

She listened raptly to Jess's Christmas message. He reminded each person there that the significance of the manger could only be understood by looking beyond this holy night, beyond the sleeping infant in the stable, to a springtime morning . . . and an empty tomb.

His benediction made Kerry's threatening tears finally spill over. She prayed silently as Jess beseeched the Lord's blessing on all within:

"And may we kneel beside the manger with singing hearts as we behold the glory of His shining presence . . . and fall before the cross with humble hearts as we behold the glory of His wondrous, endless love. . . ."

Kerry's voice was full of emotion when Jess joined her and Molly afterward. "That was a lovely Christmas service, Jess—truly, it was."

With a gentle smile, he secured the top fastener of her cape. "And you ladies look exceptionally lovely in the candlelight, too." He spoke to both of them, but Kerry knew that his eyes were on her alone. She had to drop her gaze before his for fear she'd imagine something more in his look.

"Come—I have a surprise for both of you." With Kerry on one side and Molly on the other, he led them outside to the portico, then down the steps.

Looking up when Jess came to a halt beside her, Kerry stared blankly for a moment at Cadet Sam Grant, who was standing a few feet away in the snow, a trace of a smile brightening his lightly freckled face. But it was what stood beside him that brought a gasp of delight from her.

A fine chestnut horse harnessed to a small, open sleigh, stood proudly, head high, nostrils flaring with impatience as he pawed eagerly at the snow.

"Why, Sam Grant—whatever have you been up to now?" Molly exclaimed with astonishment.

The cadet's smile grew wider as he gave Jess a conspiratorial wink. "Why, I've been carrying out Mr. Dalton's instructions, ma'am."

Kerry clapped her hands in excitement, only restraining herself at the last instant from jumping off the ground. "Oh, Jess! What a lovely surprise. Are we riding home in it?"

"That's the general idea," he said with a low chuckle. "Now, ladies, this is a two-seater, but I didn't think you'd mind bunching up a bit since it's so cold." He grinned at the happiness lighting Kerry's face as he helped her into the sleigh. Tucking her and Molly securely beneath a heavy wool lap robe, he got in beside Kerry and set the horse at a trot across the field.

Several inches of fresh snow relieved the austerity of the buildings and grounds, creating a peaceful scene much like an artist's winter landscape. The serenity of the night was broken only by the muted echo of sleigh bells draped through the harness. Kerry clenched her hands tightly, so captivated by the beauty and happiness of the night, she very nearly cried out in joy.

"Molly? Are you all right?" Jess asked, glancing at her.

"I'm perfectly fine, yes. But I am tired. If you don't mind,

Jess, I'll be needing to go directly home. Then you and Kerry can have a nice long ride, and I can go on to bed."

"Whatever you say. We don't want you to have a relapse."

When they reached the house, Kerry waited while Jess helped Molly out of the sleigh and walked with her to the door, where she stood for a moment, giving them a wave before they went on.

"Sure you're warm enough?" Jess asked as the horse resumed his trot.

"Yes, I'm fine. Oh, Jess, this is so lovely! What a nice gift it is."

He smiled, obviously pleased by her enthusiasm. "Ah, but this isn't the gift I was talking about earlier."

"But it's a wonderful gift. Whatever do you mean?"

"I mean," he replied staring straight ahead, "that you have another surprise waiting for you back at the house." He glanced over at her, his expression deceptively innocent. "Curious?"

"Of course I'm curious, and who would not be?" she exclaimed. "But surely nothing could be nicer than this," she added, huddling even closer to him.

"I won't argue with that," he said softly, wrapping her hand in his.

They rode along in contented silence, their breath making steamy clouds in the cold darkness. The stillness of the night, the warmth from the lap robe and from Jess's large body so close beside her, calmed Kerry to a sleepy daze. They had come to a full halt before she reluctantly realized their ride was over and they were home.

She looked at Jess out of eyes heavy with sleep as he came around to help her out of the sleigh. "I'm thinking," she said, her voice thick and languid, "that it would be fine if we could simply go on riding for hours and hours."

"You'd like that, would you?" he murmured, picking her

up and carrying her to the house.

"What about the horse?" she said groggily.

"He'll be fine. I've secured him, and Sam's coming by for him later."

"Do I get my other present now?" Her question was muffled against his neck.

"Mm. If you're awake enough to open it," he answered, kicking the door shut behind them and setting her down.

He helped her out of her cape, hanging it up before taking off his own coat. "Let's go into the study. I'll get a fire going."

But Molly had anticipated them. The room was already cozy with a blazing fire. Pleased, both of them moved as near to the fireplace as possible.

Kerry rubbed her arms briskly beneath the long, full sleeves of her cream-colored wool dress. "Do I get my present now?" she urged, looking very young, with her cheeks rosy from the fire's glow and her eyes bright with anticipation.

With a teasing cluck of his tongue, he scolded her in a near-flawless imitation of Molly. "Sure, and don't be so impatient, Kerry Shannon. You'll need to be waiting until I go and fetch it."

"But where is it?"

"I hid it, of course, when I came home this afternoon," he replied over his shoulder as he left the room.

When he returned, he held a long, elegantly wrapped package. Sitting down on the settee, he motioned her to join him.

"I have something for you also," she said, plopping quickly down beside him. "But Molly said I must wait until tomorrow morning to give it to you."

"Oh, yes, Molly thinks it's unforgivable to exchange gifts before Christmas Day. But I'm just selfish enough to want to be alone with you when you open this."

"Well, then, here we are . . . alone," Kerry stated matter-of-factly, reaching for the package he held on his lap.

"Wait a moment, now," he teased, holding the gift away from her. "It's rude to grab, you know."

"Oh, Jess. Stop it!"

He laughed at her impatience and handed the package to her. "All right, all right—open it."

She unwrapped it very carefully, relishing the shimmer of the fine paper draped about it. Her mouth dropped open with astonishment when the final layer parted to reveal a case, in which rested a finely crafted, solid silver flute.

With a soft gasp of wonder, she stared first at Jess, then at the flute. "Oh . . . oh, my, Jess—d'you mean . . . that this is mine?"

"Do you like it, dear?" he asked softly.

"*Like* it? It's the grandest, most beautiful thing I've ever seen! And it—it's truly for me?"

"Of course it's yours, dear. Look—your name is engraved on it." He swallowed the lump in his throat, wanting desperately to hold her, thrilled that he had made her so happy.

He knew he would always remember this moment, the way she looked, first at him, then down at the shining flute which did, indeed, bear her name. When she raised her eyes to him once more, they were shining like emeralds, glistening with happy tears. Then, placing the flute carefully in position, she blew gently across the mouth hole, testing its tone.

Slowly, a haunting, pastoral tune flowed from the beautiful instrument, its sweetness reflected in the tender joy lighting Kerry's face. With the last soft tone still echoing, she placed the precious gift at her feet, shaking her head with wonder as she studied Jess's face. Impulsively, she flung her arms around his neck. "Oh, Jess. Thank you—thank you with all my heart!"

"Say, now," he joked lightly. "I believe I rather like the way you show your gratitude. Would you fancy a piano too, dear?"

Kerry kept her arms locked about his neck, fastening a look upon him that was transparent with devotion. His broad smile faded, and the twinkle in his eyes melted to an adoring gaze. Ever so slowly, he gathered her into his arms, holding her look as he lowered his head to kiss her gently on the cheek. His breath was warm against her face as he held her snugly against him.

"You mustn't look at me that way, dear," he muttered hoarsely. "You make it very nearly impossible for me to . . ."

"To what?" she whispered against his bearded cheek.

"Kerry . . . sweet . . . you are so dear to me—"

His words were lost as he kissed her with a heartrending tenderness. When he raised his lips from hers, he gently framed her face between his hands. "You are so incredibly beautiful . . . you can't begin to imagine how happy it makes me, just to look at you." His voice broke with emotion as he pulled her even more closely to him and whispered into the soft cloud of her hair, "Happy Christmas, Kerry Shannon."

Her head seemed to fit perfectly the comfortable hollow of his shoulder as she buried her face against the fine white fabric of his shirt. With a dreamy, contented smile, she answered him. "Aye, it is that, Jess. It is indeed, thanks to you."

They sat that way a few more moments, Kerry tucked snugly inside his arm with her head resting on his shoulder, watching the fire cast its flickering shadows upon the hearth. When he finally sighed and reluctantly put her away from him, his voice was unnaturally low and smothered with emotion. "It's very late."

She nodded. "May I take the flute with me, to my room?

I want to be looking at it as I fall asleep."

He stood, drawing her to her feet but not yet releasing her from the circle of his arms. "Of course." He kissed her lightly on the forehead, then walked her to the landing of the stairway. "Good night, dear."

He watched her all the way to the top, until she went inside her room; only then did his smile fade. *You've given me many fine gifts, Lord . . . but this small girl is surely the most precious of all . . . how I cherish her, Father—but do I have the right to love her? And if I don't, how will I ever stop the loving now?*

CHAPTER FOURTEEN

Kerry stole a quick, unobserved look out the kitchen window to the back of the house where Jess was chopping firewood. His large, powerful shoulders moved smoothly beneath his old lumberman's coat as he swung the axe with broad, even strokes, occasionally stopping to brush a lock of dark hair away from his forehead with his arm and to glance contentedly about him at the crisp, white beauty of this first day of the New Year.

With a fond smile, Kerry reluctantly turned back to the stove to give the potato soup a quick stir. After checking the roast pork, she went over to the cupboard and lifted the lid off the large bowl of pickled cabbage resting on the shelf. She inhaled deeply, feeling her stomach rumble with hunger.

Today's dinner was to be special. Although he had at first refused, Jess had finally agreed to Molly's request that they invite Edmund Teague and Tom Jackson to share their

New Year's meal. Kerry puzzled again over the part of Jess and Molly's conversation she had overheard while dusting the corner shelves in the hall. A delicate, extremely valuable collection of small German china figurines that had belonged to Jess's mother—a collection Molly guarded fiercely—occupied the shelves, and Kerry had been slowly and painstakingly cleaning each one when she heard Jess and his housekeeper talking in the kitchen.

"Molly, you know I don't make a practice of inviting the cadets to eat here for any reason. If I did, you'd soon be feeding every hungry man at the Academy. There's not one of them who wouldn't jump at the chance to exchange the offerings of that mess hall for your cooking—as you well know."

"That might be true enough, Jess, but it's different with this young man, I'm thinking. He's attempted to be a friend to our lass, even if they did cause a bit of trouble for themselves. And he's alone, you know—alone for the holidays, Jess." Kerry could imagine Molly clucking her tongue and shaking her head in sympathy for poor Edmund.

"What would be the harm, having him in to share a meal? We can ask Tom Jackson as well. We should have had him in long before now to show our appreciation for the way he helped our Kerry, but with the grippe and all I simply forgot. It would be good for the lass, I'm thinking, to have the young men in. She's been shut up lately alone with us, when she should be seeing young people her own age, don't you agree?"

Kerry heard Jess clear his throat and mumble something; he sounded quite irritable, she thought. After a brief silence, he spoke again, this time a bit more kindly. "I suppose it would be all right, just for tomorrow. You do realize why I've kept young Teague away from Kerry, don't you, Molly? I could hardly condone their mischief."

Molly sounded amused when she answered. "Oh, certainly

not, Jess. Of course, their prank could not go unpunished. Still, I believe the lad has a good heart, and it's true enough he's more than fair to look upon, is he not? I must admit I've hoped for an interest to develop between the two of them. Would that be grand, now? As much for you as for them, I'm thinking. You'd have the peace of mind in knowing the lass would be well cared for without your needing to bear all the responsibility. The boy is dependable, wouldn't you say?"

"I'm not so sure that a young man who would haul your kitchen utensils out of the house in the middle of the night could be called dependable, Molly," he replied gruffly.

Irked by Molly's insinuation that it would be to everyone's benefit to have her thrust into Edmund's keeping, Kerry was irritated even more by Jess's remark. When he walked out into the hall just then, she glanced quickly down at the figurine in her hand, pretending not to notice the annoyed frown darkening his face.

"Kerry? Molly and I were wondering if you'd like to have young Teague in for New Year's dinner?" he asked shortly.

She gave him an exaggerated look of innocence and replied, "I'm sure that's your decision, not mine. Whatever you and Molly wish is perfectly fine with me."

His eyes narrowed suspiciously as he studied her. "Very well, then; we'll have him in. And Tom Jackson as well." Hesitating a moment, he finally turned and walked away, unaware of the analyzing look Molly darted at the two of them from the kitchen doorway.

Now, as Jess walked in with an armload of split logs, Kerry wondered what his mood would be this afternoon. He smiled at her as he dropped the wood into the box by the stove and went to hang up his coat on the hall hook by the door.

"Mmm . . . smells wonderful in here. Is this a combined effort, or is Molly making you practice alone on the cadets?"

"Sure, and you know Molly would never dream of allowing me to cook a holiday dinner alone, so long as she is able to walk about."

He came to stand by her at the stove, peering down into the pot of potato soup as he rolled up the sleeves of his fawn-colored shirt. "I suppose you'll be glad to see Teague again after so long a time?" He seemed extremely interested in her answer, a studied expression beneath his heavy lids.

"I suppose I will, yes. But I understand why you had to do what you did." She spooned another dab of pepper into the soup, then spooned up a taste for his approval.

"Oh, do you now? And you accept that?" She couldn't interpret the dry edge she heard in his voice, waiting as he licked the soup from his lips and nodded affirmatively.

"Of course. You did what you thought best. And I'm sure Edmund understood, also," she added, firmly moving his hand away from the pot when he tried for another spoonful.

"I'm pleased that both of you are so . . . *understanding* of my actions."

Kerry darted a slightly annoyed glance in his direction, then bent to check the custard pie in the oven. "Would you hand me that pot holder, please, Jess?"

"Do you like him very much?" he asked offhandedly as he walked over to the stove with the pad.

"Well, of course, I like him. He's my friend, isn't he?" In a much lower tone, she added, "My only friend, as a matter of fact."

With a look of displeasure, he folded his arms across his chest and demanded, "And what about Molly and me?"

His surly tone surprised her, "But you and Molly aren't friends, not really," she stammered. "You're more . . ."

He lifted a questioning brow and waited.

"What I mean is, you're more like—my family, I suppose. What I feel for you—and Molly, of course—is . . ."

140

"Yes?" he prompted quickly.

"It's special."

"I see," he muttered. "Special." Unexpectedly, he turned and stalked out of the kitchen, leaving her to wonder at his strangeness.

Their New Year's dinner was a pleasant affair. As he always did, Jess insisted that Molly dine with them. It had taken Kerry some time to get used to the idea that a gentleman would allow his servant to eat at the same table with him—or that the servant would comfortably do so. Of course, Jess never treated Molly as a servant. If anything, she appeared to fall into the role of an older sister, even a mother. But Kerry knew it would never have been allowed in the old country.

Edmund was at his cleverest that day, his droll sense of humor keeping all of them, including Jess, in continual spasms of laughter. Even Tom, serious-minded as always, allowed himself the luxury of a few smiles, although he frequently seemed uncertain as to where they should be placed.

Kerry still felt awkward around this big man who wore such a sober, unhappy expression most of the time. Her naturally sunny nature made it difficult for her to relate to his gloomy personality, but she liked and respected him. In fact, she sensed an unspoken bond between herself and Jackson. He'd been orphaned while a young boy, educated in country schools while living with relatives, and had no family status to speak of. While her rapport with him was marginal, Jess, on the other hand, appeared to be entirely comfortable with the young plebe, as though he perfectly understood his self-consciousness and was unaffected by Tom's lack of social ease. But this wasn't the first time Kerry had noticed that Jess had a gift for relating easily to others; age or education or social standing appeared to raise no barriers between him and those with whom he sought to communicate.

"So—Tom—how do you find the regime of the Academy, now that you've had a few months to settle in? Are you at home here?" Jess questioned pleasantly.

"Very much so, sir. If I can only master the academics, I'll count myself blessed."

"It's a demanding schedule, I know—takes some getting used to for most men. Are you having problems with any particular subjects?"

"Well, I struggle with French—and English grammar. To be truthful, I struggle with most all the subjects. But I like to study, sir."

Jess favored him with a look of admiration tinged with compassion. "If I can help you in any way, Tom, let me know. I'd be happy to."

He turned then to Edmund, scrutinizing him for a moment. "And you, Teague—how does it feel to have only a few months left before graduating?"

"A bit frightening, Mr. Dalton. It's home for me now. I suppose I'm anxious to get on with my life, but I'll miss the Academy."

"Oh, by the way—is the Superintendent still sending you downriver tomorrow for those land papers?"

"Yes, sir, I'm taking the afternoon steamer."

"Would you mind picking up some supplies for me while you're in the city? Some manuscript paper and a couple of books I've ordered?"

"Certainly, sir, I'd be happy to."

Molly pressed another generous slice of savory pork onto Edmund's plate. "Will you be making a career of the army Mr. Teague?"

"Yes, ma'am, that's my intention. It's what I've always dreamed of—being an army officer."

"An honorable ambition, I'm sure. But what about a wife

and family? Sure the army's not an easy way of life for them."

Kerry glanced at Jess, noticing that he seemed to have great interest in Edmund's reply.

"That's certainly true, ma'am, but it can be a very rewarding life. I hope to find a young lady who's strong enough to accept the sacrifices."

"Aye, strength is a good quality to seek in your life's partner," Molly agreed. "And do you have your special young woman chosen yet?"

Her eyes held a glint of teasing interest which Edmund matched with light banter of his own. "I know only this much for certain, ma'am: The woman I choose will have to be a great deal like you."

"Ach! Enough of that now." Flustered, she waved away his grin and rose quickly to clear the table.

Kerry got up to help, but Molly wouldn't have it. "No, now, you and Mr. Teague go along to the parlor and have a chat. You've not seen each other for a spell, so you'll be wanting to catch up a bit, I'm sure. I'll serve Mr. Jackson and Jess their coffee in the study. Perhaps you'd like to show Tom some of your materials on slavery, Jess?" she suggested with a pointed look.

Was Kerry imagining it, or did Molly sound a bit devious? Jess positively scowled at his housekeeper as he mumbled his assent, rising slowly from his chair and taking Tom with him into the study. Molly then shooed the two young people out of the dining room and into the parlor.

Kerry looked uncertainly at Edmund and gave him a weak smile as she sat down in the spoon-back chair across from him. "How have you been, then?"

"Oh, getting along," he replied, clearing his throat awkwardly before continuing. He sat rigidly straight, his back forming a perfect "L" with his hipbone, but the exactness of his military bearing failed to reach his eyes, which gleamed with customary mischief. "Did I get you in a terrible mess? You know, with the kitchen stuff?"

"Oh, no, not really. Jess—the chaplain—is a fair man, if a bit stern at times." She fiddled with a contrary curl which insisted upon flopping over her forehead. "Well, now, wasn't it kind of Molly to let me out of cleaning the kitchen so we could talk a bit?"

"Molly's playing matchmaker, you know," he said with a significant grin.

"Whatever do you mean?"

He shrugged lightly. "It's obvious. She's decided that we'd make a good pair."

Kerry's indignation was sincere. "Sure, and you're not serious."

"Sure, and I am," he teased. "Well, you can't blame Molly, you know. She doesn't realize it's all out of her hands."

"And what is *that* supposed to mean?"

His smile faded when he saw her irritation. "Molly may not have realized just yet what I have—that you've already given your heart away," he replied softly. "You don't have to pretend with me, Kerry. I know how you feel about him—and I understand. You can talk about it, if you like."

"I—I haven't the faintest notion what you're getting at, Edmund Teague," she stammered with embarrassed confusion.

"Kerry, my *friend*," he began with meaningful emphasis, "I've seen how you look at him—Mr. Dalton. And it's all right, isn't it? I mean, he isn't exactly indifferent to you, I've noticed."

"What a terrible in-insin—"

"Insinuation? I'm not implying anything wrong. I'm simply stating the obvious." He relaxed his military posture to slump down more comfortably and sling a hand over the chair arm. "You look at the man as though there's not another person alive in the entire world. And he looks at you as though he's about to choke on his own heart. Sam Grant has noticed, too."

She knew she should be offended by his bluntness, but she was more interested in his comment about the way Jess looked at her, though she pretended indifference. "That's about the silliest thing I've ever heard. If you're going to talk nonsense, I'll just go on and help Molly after all." She gathered the folds of her green and white silk skirt in her hand and started to rise from her chair, but his voice stopped her.

"What are you getting so upset about? I don't see any harm in the two of you feeling that way about each other. So the man is older than you—so what? My sister married a man fifteen years older than she is, and they have a wonderful marriage." He leaned back in his chair, keenly enjoying her renewed attention.

"You . . . you really don't think it matters, the years?" She sat back down, feeling a surge of hope.

"Why should it?" he asked, scratching his head quizzically. "The only thing that really matters is how you feel about each other, isn't it?"

"Well . . . not exactly. I mean—oh, all right. Supposing I *were* to be—fond—of Jess, just supposing. I'm not saying that I am, mind you now. But if I were, there would still be the problem of our differences, would there not?"

"Differences?" His expression was puzzled. "What kind of differences? Aside from the fact that he's a man and you're a woman—which, as I understand it, is a rather basic requirement for a good marriage."

"Oh, Edmund, don't be clever! The differences are perfectly obvious—or should be—even to you. In addition to his being thirty-two—which doesn't bother me in the least, but seems to totally stupefy him—he's a wealthy, famous man from a terribly important family." She expelled a long breath, waiting for his reaction.

"Kerry—you don't really believe any of that's important if the two of you care about each other, do you?"

She sighed, wanting to be influenced by him, but unwilling to risk it. "He's from a different world, you see," she stated softly.

"But you're now a part of his world," the cadet argued.

She shook her head sadly. "No, I'm not. I could never be a part of it. You must be born to that sort of world, I'm thinking."

He studied her seriously for a moment, then rose from his chair and walked across to her, lowering himself to the footstool in front of her. "Kerry, that's not true. What you're saying . . . it sounds as though you think you have to meet certain standards before someone can love you. That's just not how it is."

He leaned forward, intent upon making her understand. "You love someone because—well, for example, if I were in love with you, it would be because you're Kerry. Certainly any man would find it easy to love a special girl like you. . . "

Jess found them like that when he walked into the parlor, Edmund sitting at Kerry's feet, soberly attempting to make her listen to him, and Kerry bent forward, frowning with attention.

The chaplain's eyes blazed as he disarmed the cadet with a menacing glare. "Mr. Teague—"

Edmund jumped to his feet, nearly overturning the footstool. "Sir—"

There was no mistaking the warning in Jess's sharp, slicing words. "You're aware that Miss O'Neill is a minor?"

The cadet stared at him blankly.

His scowl deepening even more, Jess continued his scathing reprimand. "Even though I heard only a part of what, I'm sure, was a most interesting conversation, sir, I

146

have to tell you that you are once again sorely out of order. Correct me if you disagree, but it's my feeling that a discussion of . . . love . . . with my ward is highly inappropriate. Perhaps we'd best bring this afternoon to an end now."

Shocked into silent rage by his overbearing attitude and humiliated by his obvious misunderstanding, Kerry fled the room, nearly crashing into Molly as she turned toward the kitchen. When the concerned housekeeper would have followed her, Jess, striding purposefully down the hallway from the parlor, motioned her away.

He confronted Kerry in the kitchen, where she stood rigidly by the table, her hands splayed firmly on her hips.

"I want you to stay right here," he demanded coldly. "Once the men are gone, we're going to have a talk."

"No."

His eyes narrowed. "Kerry—" He lowered his voice, but his tightly controlled anger was still all too apparent. "I said I want to talk with you."

"But I don't want to talk with you!" She felt a spiteful dart of pleasure when she saw that she'd startled him with her defiance.

"Will you please stop acting like a child?" he grated after a moment.

"Why should I? That's what I am, after all. At least, that's how you treat me." She glanced down at the heavy pewter bowl of fruit resting in the middle of the table.

He met her statement with silence. Finally, in a considerably calmer tone, he tried again. "I'll see Teague and Jackson out. Then we'll sit down and discuss things."

She almost weakened. Even though he looked so very—military—as he stood there with his massive arms crossed over his chest and his stubborn chin jutting out further than usual, she thought she detected something else in his expression. And odd as it seemed at that particular moment, she believed for an instant she saw the

147

same tenderness in his eyes that had been there Christmas Eve when he'd given her the silver flute. But she was too shaken and far too angry to respond to it.

"If it's not asking too much, Jess," she declared icily, "I should like to be left alone. I have done nothing wrong, regardless of what you think, and we have nothing to discuss." She turned her back on him, too furious to care that she was being childishly rude.

He sighed wearily, as though he knew he was handling the entire situation badly. "You have no business allowing a young man to discuss any sort of romantic feelings with you while you're alone wit him."

She whirled around to face him. "Aha! But it's proper enough, I suppose, to discuss romantic feelings with an *older* man?"

He looked as though she'd struck him. His eyes blazed, then quickly clouded as he stood there speechless and unmoving. When he finally spoke, his voice was little more than a tight rasp. "I suppose I deserve that."

Kerry felt an immediate stab of remorse and fought quickly to undo her angry words. "Jess—it wasn't like you think with Edmund."

His face was as impassive as a stone mask, making her rush her words even more. "You heard only the end of our conversation. No matter what it may have sounded like to you, Jess, we weren't discussing anything improper. We honestly were not."

"I heard him refer to loving you—"

"No, you did not!" she snapped.

"Then what were you talking about?" he challenged.

"I—I'll not tell you that," she stammered. To tell him the truth, she would have to reveal that her feelings for him had been the subject of the conversation. That was unthinkable.

He nodded. "I see." Some niggling edge of jealousy

148

wouldn't allow him to leave it alone. "It was that innocent, was it?"

Her chin shot up, and he saw fire flash in her eyes as she gave her skirt a determined hike and raced out of the room before he could stop her.

Much later that night, in the cold gloom of his bedroom, Jess paced the wide-planked floor for over an hour before finally dropping to his knees beside the bed. With his head resting wearily on his hands, he poured out his heart to God . . .

My Lord, I can no longer lie to myself, or to You. What I feel for Kerry goes far beyond the acceptable concern of a guardian for his ward. It has nothing to do with responsibility or duty. She has become more dear to me than my own life, more precious to me than anything else in this world. I have never felt this way about another human being. I love her . . . not as a young girl who depends on me, but as a woman. Right or wrong, I can't continue to deny my feelings for her. Please—please, Lord, show me what to do. Allow me to love her openly and freely, or somehow give me the strength to put that love aside. There's such a hurt, so much pain, in trying not to love her. And worst of all, I'm hurting her as well as myself. Ah, Father, I'd rather die than hurt her, You know I would . . . help me, won't You please help me? . . .

CHAPTER FIFTEEN

While Jess was on his knees in prayer, Kerry was on her knees in front of her da's trunk. Jess had brought it back with him from New York City at Christmastime, but during the busy routine of the holiday season, Kerry had postponed her examination of its contents. She decided now to open it, with the hope that reminiscing through the things packed inside would take her mind off everything else.

Oh, Da, if you but knew what you got me into with all this, she thought ruefully, giving the top of the battered pine trunk a caressing stroke. *Here I am, beholden to a man who means the world and more to me—a man who's a star's distance beyond my reach.*

She didn't really understand Jess's anger or his unfairness. Sometimes she could almost believe that he was jealous. But was that only because she wanted to believe it? Still, there was no denying the affection he'd shown her

151

lately, at least up until today. Sure, and the man could be maddening at times. She decided she would lose no more sleep over his unpleasant behavior. *I've endured quite as many restless nights as I care to because of you, Jess Dalton, and your—your cantankerousness. Tonight I'll not be giving you a thought, and that's that.*

Pressing her lips firmly together, she slowly opened the hinges to the trunk that held all that was left of her yester-days. Old wounds of loneliness and loss were reopened as she began to sift through the items stored inside. On top were Conor's work gloves, worn pathetically thin, and his cap, which always sat at a jaunty angle on his head. With a sad smile, she traced her fingers lightly over his familiar gray shirt. When she came to his one good vest, worn only for funerals and weddings, a heaviness descended upon her, and she blinked furiously to contain the hot tears scalding her eyes.

Mrs. Glendon had carefully packed her Da's few small valuables underneath several layers of clothing. Kerry thumbed through his Bible, recalling how Conor had read it nightly, often aloud to her. Then she glanced over a note of appreciation he'd prized highly, a message from a group of dock workers he'd helped during a major dispute. There were also two precious letters from her mother, written during the weeks before she and Conor had married. Conor had allowed Kerry to read these before, but now she read them again, grateful for this slender thread binding her to the mother she'd never known.

When she came across a few letters from Mr. Andrew, Jess's father, she opened one dated only a few weeks before Conor's death. Intrigued by this correspondence between two men who had been so important in her life, she hastily scanned the first few lines.

Then her stomach knotted and her heart began to pound painfully against her chest.

. . . I want you to know that I understand why you did what you did, Conor. Still, the money was taken from the labor union treasury, and they aren't going to sweep that under the rug. While I cannot condone your actions, I will do everything within my power to help you. I do fear, however, that you are correct in believing that your arrest is imminent. Once the investigation by the union's attorneys is complete, they'll waste no time . . .

Whatever could this be? What investigation . . . what arrest? She read on, feeling more and more ill by the moment.

I know you've hoped to keep this from your daughter, but you can no longer put off telling her everything. The shock will be much, much worse for her if you wait too long—you must tell her the truth, Conor, and tell her now. Naturally, she'll be hurt; but I've witnessed her love for you, and I do not believe for a moment that anything—no matter how grievous it might be—can destroy that love . . .

Rest assured that, should anything happen to me, my son, Jess, has been fully informed of the guardianship agreement, as well as your situation with the theft, and is perfectly willing to be responsible for Kerry as long as necessary. Jess is a fine young man, so I hope it gives you some peace of mind to know that either he or I will see to your beloved daughter if the need should ever arise, God forbid . . .

Although imprisonment is a definite possibility, you musn't despair: There are many things we can do to avoid that fate. Be assured that we will exercise every option available to us. We'll talk about this more next time we meet—I plan to be in Buffalo within just a few weeks, and we'll discuss everything then. Until then, my friend, try not to worry—but do talk with Kerry. . . .

Money taken from the union treasury . . . arrest . . . imprisonment? She looked up from the letter, her eyes wild and stricken. The grief she'd felt only moments before now

153

quickly fled, leaving her emotions in a turmoil of shock, despair, and bewildered anger.

Her beloved da a thief? The man she'd looked up to as a giant all her life, the very man who had disciplined her for so much as a tiny fib when she was still a small girl, who had assured her time and time again throughout her childhood that "the honest way is the only way"—this man had stolen, had been saved from imprisonment only by his sudden death? And she hadn't known, hadn't even guessed?

But Jess knew. Of course, he knew. Mr. Andrew would have told him the whole story once he learned he was dying, because of the guardianship agreement. The pain battering at her mind and heart roared to a sudden, devastating climax of humiliation. Dear heaven, to think she had boasted about the honor of their family, the integrity of Conor O'Neill, repeating to Jess her da's frequent reminder: "It isn't poverty that bows a man's head, lass— it's dishonesty. So long as a man lives by the truth, he lives with honor."

She felt her stomach wrench. How pathetic she must have seemed to Jess when he'd known all along that there was no honor in the O'Neill name. *Oh, Da, how could you do this? How could you . . . and not even say a word of warning to me?*

With the back of one hand, she wiped furiously at the tears on her cheeks. The awful significance of what she had just learned hurled itself violently against her heart, and her faced paled with shame. No wonder Jess had been so angry with her and Edmund the night he caught them taking the utensils from the kitchen. *More than likely he feared I'd inherited Da's tendency toward theft.*

Whatever shall I do now? I can't stay here, of course. Oh, dear Lord, I can't even bear the thought of facing him again, knowing what he must think of Da . . . and me. Sure, and I'll not be taking another cent from him for my keep.

He's done what he's done because of his promise to his father, and because he's a fine, decent man. But it must stop here and now.

She knew she had to get away as soon as possible. It had been difficult enough before, caring so deeply for Jess and with him so determined not to allow any closeness to grow between them. But now it would be impossible. This awful thing made a mockery of any hope she might have had that Jess could ever love her. Perhaps his silence had been meant to protect her, but his kindness only deepened her humiliation.

Drained, she rocked slowly back and forth on her knees, her arms clasped tightly against her chest as though she could keep the leaden ball of unhappiness inside her from escaping. When she finally rose to her feet, it was very late, and the house was silent. She walked stiffly to the bedroom door, opened it quietly, and stepped out into the hall. Overcome with a need to get out of the house, she started down the stairs. Perhaps a walk around the yard in the cold night air would help clear her head so she could decide what she was going to do.

Thinking Jess and Molly had retired long ago, she took her cape from the hallway closet and went to the kitchen to get the boots she'd left by the door earlier that day. She caught a quick breath of surprise and stopped just inside the room. Jess sat at the table, illuminated only by a small beeswax candle as he leaned his head wearily upon one hand.

Hearing her startled gasp, he looked up, blankly at first, then with a fast-dawning awareness. Kerry abruptly turned to leave, but his voice stopped her. "No, Kerry—stay." In a much softer tone, he added, "Please, stay with me." He was beside her before she could get away.

"I—I didn't know anyone was up. I just came down to—"

As though he sensed she was about to run from him, he reached out and held her gently by the forearm. "You couldn't sleep either?"

When she didn't answer, he moved to guide her over to one of the chairs at the table, but she resisted him. "Kerry, please, sit down. We have to talk. There's something you need to know, something I have to explain."

He's going to tell me now? After all this time? But why? To shame me into more proper behavior? Why now?

"It—it's late, Jess. I'm a bit weary, I think. Could we not wait until tomorrow?"

"I've waited entirely too long as it is," he answered quietly. His hand still clasped her arm as his eyes searched hers. "You deserve an explanation, Kerry, as to why I sometimes . . . behave as I do, especially regarding Edmund Teague."

"I told you I understood," she said quickly, trying to keep her voice from breaking.

"But you couldn't have," he protested. "Not really. Because I was never truthful with you. Kerry, dear . . . listen to me." His face was close as he tipped her chin with one finger to make her raise her eyes to him. "There's so much you need to know. Perhaps you won't like what you hear—it may even turn you away from me. But I have to take that chance."

Turn her away from him? Nothing could have turned her away from him, not ever, she thought miserably, *except the shame that had become hers this night.* She tried in vain to avoid his gentle, searching gaze, but he firmly cupped her chin in his hand and forced her to look at him.

His voice was threaded with remorse and fatigue as he spoke. "I've been so unfair to you about Edmund. I know you didn't understand why; most of the time, I didn't understand it myself. But you see, there's a reason I've been so—possessive. I've been afraid to tell you. I wasn't sure I had the right. But I know now that I must."

Pain seared her heart when she saw how terribly tired and discouraged he appeared to be. "Please, Jess, not now. I—" She tried to squirm free of his grasp, but he continued to hold her.

"Kerry—listen to me. I need to say this—I can't keep it locked inside me any longer. I'll understand if you want to get away from me then, but at least hear me out."

"No! I won't listen to you." The delicate strand of her self-control snapped, and she tried to pull away from him.

He held her, but not so firmly now, and there was a stricken look in his eyes that Kerry knew she would never forget. "I'm sorry," he said quietly, his voice thick with emotion. "Oh, Kerry . . . I'm so sorry. I've frightened you—I never meant to do that. I thought . . . perhaps you realized, at least had some idea, after—" He shook his head. "Had I known I'd upset you this much, I would never have—"

With one last agonized look at him, she jerked free and fled the room, blinded by the tears swimming in her eyes. *Perhaps I'm as childish as he believes me to be,* she thought bitterly as she ran up the stairs to the security of her bedroom, *but I cannot bear the shame of hearing this from his lips.* She slammed the door shut, gasping for breath as she leaned heavily against it.

You had to force it, didn't you? Jess thought, staring out the window into the dark night that seemed to represent the desolate coldness of his heart. *You had to inflict yourself on her, try to resolve everything so you'd finally have some peace . . . well, what peace will you have now? You frightened her, drove her away from you . . . and small wonder . . . she's eighteen years old, forced into a situation she never wanted—insecure, dependent upon a big, clumsy, crashing bore who can't keep his hands off her or a civil tongue in his head. What did you expect? You've ruined everything—everything . . . you're never going to see that look you love so much in her eyes again, man . . . the look that made you feel ten feet tall. That was fear you just saw— fear, or, even worse, revulsion. You fool, you inconsiderate, blind fool. . . .*

With a tormented, self-mocking smile, he recalled Molly's words of no more than an hour ago, when she'd found him alone in the kitchen, in an obvious agony. She had charged through his barrier of reserve with some pointed, concerned questions.

After hearing his admission of love for Kerry—and the guilt he'd been suffering for weeks because of his feelings—Molly had ventured a rare observation. "I'm thinking perhaps your loving the lass might be a fine thing after all, Jess. Do you not have a deep concern for her and for her welfare? What better way could you be finding to care for her proper and look after her future than by making her your wife? Sure, and a few years need not be such a problem."

At first he could only stare dumbly at her, but when the tempting thought broke through that there might be some logic to her words, he asked, his voice faltering weakly, "But . . . what if she doesn't *want* me?"

"Then she will tell you so," Molly declared with unnerving bluntness. "But, Jess, lad," she went on, softening her tone, "what if she *does* want you? Should you not be finding out for yourself?"

Well, Molly, he thought bitterly, a glazed look of hopelessness settling over his face, *it would seem that I have my answer. . . .*

CHAPTER SIXTEEN

By the time Kerry went downstairs the next morning, she was relieved to find that Jess had already left the house; she knew her resolve to leave would weaken if she were to see him again. This was the day Edmund was to go to New York City, and she had decided during the night that it would also be the day she left West Point for good, if she could only convince Edmund to help her.

First, however, she had to find a way to talk with the young cadet. The apprehensive pounding of her heart increased as she realized she had no choice but to slip by Molly and make her way to the dock to wait for Edmund.

She made a pretense of doing her housework until early afternoon, trying to keep up a normal flow of conversation with Molly, who kept insisting that Kerry looked "sickly." Knowing her only sickness was of the heart, Kerry avoided the housekeeper as much as possible.

When she finally began to pack, she hurriedly put into

her worn valise only those few items of clothing and meager personal effects she had when she arrived, deliberately ignoring the fine new things Jess had bought for her. She glanced with an aching heart at her cherished leather boots, remembering the pleasure that had glinted in his eyes when he gave them to her. She swallowed hard to choke back the sob in her throat before setting the boots inside the wardrobe, out of sight.

Tugging relentlessly at the back of her mind the whole time she was packing was the thought of her new silver flute. She knew what she must do, of course, but she waited as long as possible before picking it up for the last time, squeezing her eyes tightly shut for a moment to hold back the tears. Her features were ravaged with despair as she stroked the perfect lines of the flute once more, then placed it very gently upon the window seat and turned away from it, knowing she could put the instrument behind her, but never the memory of Jess's face on Christmas Eve, so tender and warm and caring. Or so she had thought.

Finished at last, she tucked the valise behind the bedroom door, then went quietly downstairs to determine Molly's whereabouts. The thought of the strict but softhearted housekeeper who had mothered her so willingly—and so well—during the past few months caused an intense wave of fresh pain to wash over her. She would miss Molly—almost as much as she'd miss Jess.

When she reached the hall landing, she could hear Molly's soft humming in the parlor at the front of the house. Knowing she had the opportunity to leave by the kitchen door without being seen, Kerry quickly grabbed her cape from the hall closet and hurried back upstairs. Throwing on her cape, she picked up her valise from behind the door, then tiptoed down the steps as softly as possible and left the house.

At the edge of the yard, she turned for one last look at

the house that been home to her for the past few months—happy months, for the most part. With a sense of sorrow beyond tears, she hurried across the field, her shoulders hunched against the wind. Descending the hilly, snow-covered path to the dock was a challenge for her; she slipped frequently, completely losing her balance and falling once, going to her knees in the snow.

By the time she finally reached the dock, she was biting her lips to control the sobs of frustration and anguish rising in her throat. She sat down on her valise to wait for Edmund, ignoring the curious stare of an army officer who appeared to be waiting for the steamer that had just docked.

Less than half an hour later, she saw Edmund hurrying toward the dock. When he was close enough to recognize her, he exclaimed sharply, "Kerry! What's wrong? What in the world are you doing here?"

"Shh! I have to talk to you, Edmund—quickly." She grasped his arm and began a frantic appeal to him in a low, hoarse voice.

"You must take me with you—I *have* to go with you. I'll explain when we get aboard, Edmund—just help me, please."

"Are you out of your mind, Kerry? Do you know what will happen to both of us if I take you on board that boat? What is it? What's happened?"

"Edmund Teague, you told me if I ever needed a favor I could depend on you," Kerry rasped, trying to keep her voice low. "Well, I need your help *now*. I got myself in a whole parcel of trouble for you once, did I not? Now I need you to help me—will you or won't you?" She hissed the words at him, her eyes blazing with impatience.

The bewildered cadet, casting a quick, uneasy glance around them, leaned down to whisper desperately, "I'll be dismissed if they catch us. Why do you want to leave anyway? Does Mr. Dalton know where you are?"

161

"*No!*" she snapped, pulling her valise up under her arm. "Well, Mr. Teague, I am going to New York—with or without your help—so please let me by."

Grabbing her arm when she tried to move around him, Edmund tugged her back to his side. "All right—all right. If it's that important, come on. But you'd better have an awfully good reason for this."

Fortunately, they were the only ones boarding the steamboat, so they went unnoticed, even by the pilot, who was carrying on a rather heated conversation with the same army officer who'd been staring curiously at Kerry before Edmund arrived.

"There's ice on the river," Kerry observed, gripping the rail tightly as the steamer began to back away from the dock. "We won't have trouble getting to New York, will we?"

"No, it's not frozen yet—though it will be by next week if this weather keeps up." Turning to her, he demanded, "Now, then, suppose you just explain what's going on."

She glanced away from him, unwilling to meet his scrutiny. "I—I found out something that makes it impossible for me to stay here. I'm going to the city and get a job. I have to make my own way from now on."

"You're crazy!" he exploded, grabbing her by the elbow to make her face him. "What could be so bad that you'd leave Mr. Dalton and Molly like this? If I'd known you had anything as wild as this in mind, I never would have—" He stopped abruptly, making her squirm under the penetrating study of his dark eyes.

But when he spoke again, his voice was teasing, as though he hoped to blow to the wind this whole escapade. "What'd you do, murder someone?"

"Stop that, Edmund. It's not funny." Furious at the mist she felt clouding her eyes, she pulled away from his grasp. "You wouldn't understand it even if I explained. All I'm

162

asking of you is to help me find a place to stay until I can get a position somewhere."

"What kind of position? What can you do?" Leaning heavily against the rail, he pulled off his cap and ran a nervous hand through his hair. "Kerry, you're much too young to be on your own in a place like New York. You have no idea what it's like for—well, for immigrants. Especially for pretty young Irish girls. It's not safe."

"Oh, don't be daft! I'm perfectly able to take care of myself, thank you." Her chin went up as her eyes glinted with fiery indignation. "I can go into service, that's what I can do, and I'll not be needing to depend on *anyone* for my keep."

Shaking his head helplessly, Edmund groaned. "I can't believe this. I'm just a few months—*months*—away from graduation and here I am, most likely throwing the last three years right down the river for you."

Her expression changed as she realized for the first time the position in which she'd placed her friend. "Oh, Edmund, I *am* sorry. I don't want to be the cause of your getting into trouble. Sure, and I wasn't thinking of anyone but myself."

"Oh . . . it'll work out, I suppose," he muttered, his frown fading. "Probably no one will ever know." His voice weakened even more when he added, "Until Mr. Dalton finds out."

"Jess won't be caring that much; you needn't worry," she muttered bitterly.

"Ha!" he snorted. "You really *are* out of your mind if you believe *that*."

"I don't want to talk about it any more. It's over and done with, and that is that." She thrust out her chin with determination, lifting her face to the spray from the water.

The cadet's look held disapproval as well as a question. "You could at least tell me why you're leaving."

He was right, of course; she owed him that much. And so she proceeded to tell him the whole story, her voice tear-smothered but firm. By the time she had finished, a resigned tiredness had settled over her, deadening her eyes and paling her complexion.

Edmund studied her with concern for a long moment before attempting to reason with her. "Kerry—I must say this—please don't get angry. You're not thinking clearly about all this. You should have taken some time, talked to the chaplain—or Molly, at least."

Too tired to be angry, she merely stared at him as he continued.

"Whatever your father may have done, he must have had a good reason. From what you've told me about him, he wasn't a man to do this sort of thing out of greed. Perhaps if you'd just talk to Mr. Dalton, he'd be able to explain why—"

"*No!* Can't you understand? My da was a *thief!*"

"All right. What if he was? Why should you have to pay for his mistake? Don't you want to stay at the Point?"

"Oh, Edmund," she said with a weary sigh, "it isn't a matter of what I want or don't want. I'm simply a problem Da pushed off onto a kindhearted man too decent to refuse him. He, in turn, passed me on to his son. Now I must free Jess of the burden I've been and make my own way. That's all there is to it. Please don't make me talk about it any longer."

It was almost dusk when they docked at New York City. Edmund lifted the valise under one arm, pulling Kerry firmly along beside him with his other hand.

"I have a cousin who works at a residential hotel on the East Side; I think he'll help us. He might even be able to get you a job if you're really determined to go through with this."

"I must," she said quietly. "But I do see now I shouldn't

164

have involved you, Edmund. It's going to go badly for you, isn't it? I'm sorry—I truly am." She looked at him anxiously, squinting her eyes against the icy snow pelting her face.

A variety of emotions paraded across his good-natured features as he looked down at her. "Look, forget about that part of it. It'll work out. We're friends, and you'd do it for me, I know. Come on now—let's hurry. It's freezing out here."

They rushed along the narrow streets, huddling together to draw warmth from each other. "Listen, Kerry, don't expect too much from this hotel. It's nothing fancy—just a kind of boardinghouse. But it's clean, and the neighborhood isn't too bad. Kenneth, my cousin, is a decent guy, too; you can trust him."

The enormity of what she'd done was just beginning to weigh upon her. "I'm sure it will be fine, Edmund; don't worry." Her voice was faint, her thoughts elsewhere. She was tired, cold, and miserable, and there would be no respite from any of it. She faced an empty night, an empty future.

I won't be seeing Jess again, she thought with a sense of loss so great it seemed to crush her. *I won't be going to his study tonight, won't be hearing his rich, fine voice explaining all those wonderful books to me as he used to . . . . I won't sit in front of the fire with him again, or feel the roughness of his coat against my cheek or the softness of his beard . . . . I will never see him again . . . .*

Angry because of the self-pity she'd given in to, Kerry deliberately forced herself to concentrate on her surroundings. In spite of the roaring wind and snow, the narrow streets were fairly crowded with people rushing here and there. Kerry heard her native Gaelic and a number of unfamiliar languages all along the way. It was a parade of nationalities and races; she saw black faces, red and yellow faces. Some were in tatters, while others were dressed like

165

royalty. For the most part, the crowds were rude and loud and frenzied. They passed taverns, small shops, and restaurants, all tossing their own particular sounds and smells out into the street among the tenements and the tall buildings with brick fronts strung together in rows.

Kerry felt threatened by the towering buildings and the noisy confusion around her. She'd been in New York only once, the day she took the steamer to West Point, so it was all new and strange to her. She wondered uneasily how many more new experiences she might have to face before she could find peace for herself.

A rough voice directly in front of her startled her out of her thoughts. "Found yourself a nice little Irish wench, did you, soldier-boy? Be a good fellow and share, won't you?"

Kerry leaned into Edmund involuntarily, her eyes wide surprise and panic. The man blocking their way was big, with a red, swollen face and eyes that made her feel dirty and threatened.

Edmund stared directly into the bully's small round eyes. His voice was harsh and level as he ordered him to move. "Push off, mister, before you get hurt."

Their tormentor made a move toward the much smaller cadet, but Edmund was smooth on his feet and quick as a cat. Stuffing his hand up against the man's face, he poked at his eyes and forced him back against a brick storefront, then doubled him over with a sturdy punch in the stomach.

Moving swiftly, before the man had time to recover himself, Edmund grabbed Kerry and began to run, pulling her along with him. "Come on—let's get out of here!"

Once they had put several blocks between them and the man who'd accosted them, Edmund stopped, glancing down at Kerry with concern. "You all right?"

Shaken by the ugly scene and thought of what could have happened, Kerry's voice was uncertain when she answered. "Yes . . . I'm fine. Let's go on."

It seemed forever before she heard Edmund say, "Here we are." He led her quickly across the street to an odd-shaped building. Kerry thought it resembled an enormous piece of pie, but the windows glowed with light. For the present at least, it represented safety.

Hurrying up to the porch, they brushed off the snow and entered the small plainly furnished lobby of the hotel. The clerk behind the desk, a tall, stout man with thinning brown hair and friendly dark eyes, glanced up. His face broke into a wide smile. "Why, Edmund! Whatever are you doing here on a night like this?" His gaze moved to Kerry with an unspoken question.

"Kenneth, how are you?" Taking Kerry by the arm, Edmund led her closer to the desk. "Kenneth, this is a very good friend of mine, Miss Kerry O'Neill. She needs a room for a few days. She's also interested in finding a position in the city. Do you think you could help her?"

Edmund's cousin hesitated before answering, but he continued to smile. "If you don't mind a very simple room, Miss O'Neill, we have a few vacancies. As for a job, are you interested in a specific type of position?"

"A simple room is all I want, sir, and I'd be extremely grateful for any job I can find. I can cook and clean. I'm a hard worker, and I can read and write well, too."

"Kerry—Miss O'Neill—is from Buffalo, Kenneth. She's not exactly sure just yet how long she'll need a room, but can you trust me for it until I can borrow a bit from home?"

Kerry started to protest. Then she suddenly realized with dismay that she had no money—not a cent. There was nothing to do except let Edmund help her once again.

"That's fine, Edmund," his cousin assured him. "We might have a position for you right here in the hotel, Miss O'Neill," he said, turning to Kerry, "if you're a good cook. I believe one of the kitchen helpers is moving away next week."

"Oh, I'm a good cook, sir. I had a fine teacher, I did—no one knows more about a kitchen than Molly Larkin."

Kenneth gave them keys, one for Kerry and another for Edmund, whose room would be directly across the second-floor hall from Kerry's. When they stepped inside her room and lighted the candles in the wall sconces, Kerry surveyed it with a sinking feeling in her stomach.

It was oppressively small, crowded with a bed, a dresser, a wardrobe, a small worn divan, one chair, and a thread-bare rug. No niceties such as she'd grown used to, nothing to give it a bit of charm like her room at home.

Home! She no longer had a home—not in Buffalo, not at West Point. This small, depressing room was her home now. *And so it is,* she conceded firmly. *And I'll be making the best of what I have. At least it will be a roof over my head and a shelter from the cold.*

She added a quick, silent prayer. *I'm sorry—Lord—I seem to be doing a great deal of complaining lately. Sure, and You've already given me more than some of my people will ever see in a lifetime. I need to be thanking You, not whimpering to myself.*

She squared her shoulders and turned to Edmund. "Well, now, this is very nice, isn't it? And I will certainly pay you back, Edmund, just as soon as I get to working—I promise."

With a nonchalant shrug, he smiled at her. "Don't worry about it, Kerry. Let's go downstairs and see if we can get some dinner—I'm starved, aren't you? You can unpack later."

"When will you leave?" she asked, suddenly anxious at the thought of being entirely on her own.

"I'll have to be back at the Point by day after tomorrow."

"Oh . . . yes . . . of course you will. Edmund—will they really make you leave the Academy? Jess will know, won't he, that we left together, that you helped me?"

He forced a lopsided grin, replacing the worried look he'd worn all evening. "I suppose I could get lucky—perhaps the firing squad will be on furlough this week."

"Oh, Edmund." Tears of misery welled up in her eyes. "I am sorry."

"Will you *stop* that? I'll be all right. Now, come on—unless you want to add a dead man in your room to your other troubles. I can't last much longer without some food."

It was a night Kerry would never forget, the longest night she'd even known. There was no sleep for her, no forgetting where she was or where she'd been.

The room was cold, and her heart was colder. Huddled miserably beneath the few blankets afforded each occupant, she sought a warmth that didn't exist. *You needn't be looking for warmth any longer, Kerry O'Neill,* an inner voice nagged at her. *There will be no warmth for you anywhere for a long, long time . . . not without Jess's smile.*

Every time she closed her eyes, she saw his face—that strong, dear face she'd grown to love more than life—and just when she approached an uneasy slumber, she'd see his deep blue eyes staring at her, startling her into a guilty wakefulness.

She tried to stiffen herself against the strange night sounds of the city, shivering in the darkness as she wondered what the future held for her, trying to pray, but finding even that solace out of reach. The only words that would come sounded like weak mews of self-pity. She feared she'd simply annoy the good Lord with her sniveling.

By the time the first light of morning began to brighten the room, she was numbly repeating the words to an Irish lullaby her brother Liam had taught her when they were small:

"Someone's beside me, someone's above me, someone's near by me to keep and to love me. . . ."

Oh, Father, please . . . please don't let Jess hate me. . . .

CHAPTER SEVENTEEN

While Edmund attended to his errands for the Superintendent the next day, a despondency unlike any she'd ever known gripped Kerry. The anguish of missing Jess and Molly intensified her guilt and sharpened her worry about Edmund. Perhaps she should have waited a day or so and left the Point by herself, but she would have been at a total loss in knowing what to do once she arrived in New York City alone. Still, she'd been unforgivably selfish. . . .

Her depression deepened when she thought about Jess's anger. He would never understand why she'd done this. He would simply be more positive than ever that she was an ungrateful, rebellious child. Ah, but what did it matter now what Jess might think? She'd not be seeing him again anyway.

Seeking comfort in her da's Bible, which she'd tucked inside her valise at the last moment, she whispered the words of the Fifty-seventh Psalm again, her lips trembling as she read:

Be merciful unto me, O God, be merciful unto me: for my soul trusteth in thee: yea, in the shadow of thy wings will I make my refuge, until these calamities be overpast.

By the time Edmund finally returned, the room was gloomy with the approach of evening. Kerry almost stumbled and fell in her eagerness to let him in.

"Oh, Edmund, I was getting so worried for you. Did you get the things the Superintendent wanted?"

Removing his cap as he entered, the cadet placed some parcels on the divan and began to shrug out of his coat. "Yes, it's all taken care of. What have you been doing with yourself all day? Did you hear anything from Kenneth about a job yet?"

"No—d'you think we should talk with him again?" A worried frown creased her forehead.

"Probably wouldn't be a bad idea—in case he forgot," he said, brushing his hair back from his forehead and hanging his coat in the small wardrobe.

"Kerry, you haven't had anything to eat all day, have you?" He gave her a quick glance of concern.

"Oh, it doesn't matter. I don't believe I could have eaten anyway," she replied tightly.

"Kerry—are you still sure you want to go through with this?" he questioned anxiously. "It's not too late to go back, you know. I'll go to Mr. Dalton with you and help you explain—"

"No, I can never go back, Edmund. What's done is done—please, let's don't talk about it anymore. I have to look ahead now, not behind."

"Well, I still think you're wrong," he muttered, exasperated. "Mr. Dalton seems to care so much for you—"

His protest was cut short by a knock at the door. "That's probably Kenneth now." Edmund tossed her some matches before turning the doorknob. "Light those candles, why don't you? It's getting dark in here."

But the gloom of the Spartan room was nothing compared with the dark anger that clouded the face of the large man standing in the hallway when Edmund opened the door.

"Mr. Dalton! S-sir!"

Kerry stood, her back to the door as she reached upward to one of the candle sconces with a lighted match in her hand. She froze like a statue until the flame began to lick at her fingers. Blowing out the match with a shaky breath, she remained where she was, staring at the wall and clenching both hands tightly together in front of her. Her heart banged against her rib cage as a churning mixture of dread and hope surged through her.

"Kerry!" His voice cracked out her name like a shot.

Slowly she forced herself to turn around and face him, keenly aware of the clamminess of her hands. Her mouth went dry when she fixed her eyes on the tall, rigid, black-clad figure standing in the doorway. He looked for all the world like an angry Old Testament prophet about to vent his wrath. She fastened her eyes deliberately on his boots as he walked in and stopped just a few steps over the threshold to stand ominously still, saying nothing. Kerry could hear the uneven rasp of his breathing, not knowing whether it was from the cold evening air or the heat of his anger.

When she could stand it no longer, she finally raised her eyes. What she saw there set off a warning bell in her head. His jaw was locked relentlessly, his chin set in an obstinate thrust. But his eyes were the worst. The contemptuous fury in them, combined with another emotion she couldn't discern, dashed any hope she might have had that he was going to be reasonable.

Edmund made a noble attempt to divert the chaplain's attention from Kerry. "Mr. Dalton, sir, please let me explain—"

Without so much as a glance, Jess silenced him with words sharp enough to slice. *"Get out!"*

"Don't, Jess!" Kerry cried out. "None of this is his—"

Ignoring her, Jess pivoted his large body around toward the cadet and harshly grated out a threatening command. "You *move,* Mister! *Get downstairs and wait there for me!"*

"No!" Jess whirled around in surprise when he heard the unexpected strength in Kerry's voice. "Don't you treat him like that, Jess Dalton. He's done no wrong except what I begged him to do—that's the truth, now. The only thing he's guilty of is helping me!"

"Helping you?" he challenged incredulously. "Helping you to do what? Drive me mad with worry and put Molly back to bed with grief? Disgrace yourself and the honor of the Academy? What in the name of heaven were the two of you thinking of?"

Suddenly, unexpectedly, the hardness of his features seemed to shatter, crumbling to an expression of bewilderment and despair. With a wretched feeling of guilt, Kerry encountered the pain in his eyes.

"Why did you do this? Why run away like—criminals?" His voice, softer now, was thick with distress and confusion, and a sharp needle of regret stabbed at Kerry's heart when she noticed that his hand trembled as he raked it through his hair.

"If the two of you are in love, if you wanted to be together, couldn't you have come to me and told me? You—you could have been married," he said quietly, looking away from them, "after graduation. How could you do this—to me, to Molly—to yourselves?"

The silence of the room hovered like a heavy mist around Kerry's wild, hammering pulse. Her green eyes clouded with confusion for a moment, then slowly widened in astonished disbelief as the meaning of his words sank in.

"In *love?* Edmund . . . and I? Whatever are you thinking—"

"Sir, you couldn't be more wrong," Edmund broke in urgently. "It's nothing like that—we're not in love. We—"

Jess turned wounded, puzzled eyes first to the cadet, then to Kerry. In a voice that betrayed inner torment, he rasped, "Then what are you doing here . . . together like this?"

"Oh, Jess!" Kerry cried out with the force of shocked humiliation. "Edmund was only helping me to get away, he was. It's nothing like what you're thinking! He's my friend—we aren't—"

"Mr. Dalton?" Edmund spoke quietly, but firmly. "Sir, I believe you need to talk with Kerry alone. Please, sir—I'll wait downstairs." Without giving Jess time to reply, he grabbed his coat from the wardrobe and left the room.

They stood staring at each other for a long time, neither willing to break the tension. Finally he gave in to the brave, though guarded expression on her face and slowly unbuttoned his greatcoat, shrugging it wearily from his shoulders.

"All right . . . if there's anything you want to explain, I'm willing to listen."

She wished he'd sit down instead of standing there, looking so big and formidable. But he remained fixed where he was, his hands on the back of the chair where he'd draped his coat.

"How did you find us?" she questioned hesitantly.

His words were emotionless. "An officer saw you getting on the steamer together. Once he described Teague, I had only to check his file to see where he might take you in New York."

When she volunteered nothing, he broke the silence with a pointed, "I'm waiting, Kerry."

"I—I simply thought it was time to free you of your . . . responsibility for me. I made Edmund take me with him on the steamer."

He sighed deeply, interrupting her. "Try again."

"W—what d'you mean?"

He moved closer to her and pushed her, not roughly, but deliberately, down onto the divan. "Edmund Teague is a head taller than you and a great deal stronger. You didn't make him do anything. Now, you tell me the *truth*. Why did you leave?" He towered over her, making her feel diminished and intimidated by his very size and the warning in his voice.

She looked up at him, her eyes eyes blazing defiantly as a new wave of anger boiled over inside her. It was his fault, after all, that the truth had been kept from her. "All right, then. I found out about my da—what he did."

The look that met her outburst was blank. "Your da? What are you talking about?"

"The money!" she exclaimed impatiently. "The funds he—he stole from the labor union. I was going through his things in the trunk and found a letter Mr. Andrew had written to him."

She jumped to her feet, crying out in frustration, "Oh, Jess—why couldn't you have told me? Why did you let me go on believing he was what I thought he was?"

"Wait." He put out a hand to stop her rush of words. "What letter are you talking about? What did it say?"

Baffled by his attitude, she hesitated. Was he going to try to keep her in the dark, even now? "Your father wrote to Da about what he'd done, telling him he'd help him all he could, that he understood why he'd . . . stolen . . . the money, even though he couldn't excuse it."

Frowning, Jess reached out to touch her shoulder. "Is that all he said? No more?"

"Just that—that you would be responsible for me if

176

something should happen to him, to your father. Why?"

He searched her eyes with what appeared to be genuine confusion. "This letter—when was it written?"

"A few weeks before Da died." *Why did it matter?*

"And you left because of that?" He moved slightly closer to her, his hand still on her shoulder. "Because of that letter?"

"Well, not only that, no. But I could not stay there with you any longer, don't you see, after learning that Da was a—a thief." She clenched her hands tightly together as she lowered her head, unable to go on meeting his penetrating gaze.

"But why?"

She looked at him sharply, not understanding. "What do you mean?"

"Why should you feel the need to leave because of something your father had done?" His voice was measurably lower, though still insistent.

"Well, because—because that was all I had to make me . . . worthy, don't you see?"

"No," he said softly. "I'm afraid I don't." He moved to the couch and drew her down beside him. "Tell me what you mean, Kerry. Tell me exactly what you mean."

But she didn't know how. "I—well, as long as I had the—the honor of my family, I thought perhaps it might not matter too much about my not being a lady—like your Miss Emily," she said in a tone little more than a whisper.

"Emily?" Surprise pitched his voice higher than usual. "What does Emily have to do with any of this? How do you know about her?"

Realizing too late that she'd said far too much, that now she'd have to explain herself, Kerry bit anxiously at her lower lip. "I—I can't tell you any more."

"You must tell me," he insisted. "What about Emily?" His eyes burned into her.

Raising one hand as though to shield her eyes from him, she finally spoke. "Molly told me all about her—what a fine lady she was—and how you loved her . . . and about the accident and how you've missed her all this time . . ." Her words drifted off awkwardly.

"But what does any of that have to do with your father—and your leaving?" He reached over and gently cupped her chin in his big hand, forcing her to look at him.

"Tell me, Kerry."

"Oh, please, Jess. I don't want to say any more."

Grasping her slender shoulders in his hands, he refused to let her look away from him. He saw her humiliation and misery, and hated himself for exposing it—but he was desperate to hear the rest. He must have the truth, all of it.

Kerry caught her breath in surprise when she saw that his anger was gone. In its place was an odd glint of something akin to hope. And a question.

Resigned, finally, to the inevitability of his knowing her feelings, she gave him a pleading look. "I wanted to be . . . fine enough for you, don't you see? I knew I could never be wealthy or change my station in life, but I thought with you educating me and with my family being honorable, however poor, it might be enough . . . ."

"Enough for what, Kerry?" his soft voice urged her.

The stricken look in her eyes deepened as she whispered, "Enough for you to love me."

His hands tightened almost painfully on her shoulders as his heart began to thud violently against his chest. "To love you?" he repeated in a harsh whisper, his head reeling crazily with all sorts of hopeful, impossible thoughts.

She nodded sadly. "I'm sorry, Jess. I know you never wanted me to feel . . . to feel that way about you, but I simply couldn't help it—it just happened. And sometimes I hoped . . . that is—" She flushed miserably, then tried to lower her burning face into her hands so he wouldn't see her shame.

But he refused to let her look away from him, lifting her chin firmly to search her face. "How did you feel?"

The blaze in his eyes and the catch in his voice made her breath choke convulsively in her throat. "What do you mean?"

"What kind of feeling are you talking about, Kerry, this feeling you had for me?"

"You know," she whispered, feeling mortified and foolish.

But Jess was smiling . . . smiling and shaking his head slowly. "Tell me," he demanded.

"Oh, Jess . . . I loved you . . . surely you know how I loved you . . . ." She turned her head away, embarrassed anew by tears spilling onto her cheeks.

"Loved me, Kerry?" he prompted softly, in a voice that seemed to come from a distant tunnel. "And now?"

"Now?"

"How do you feel about me now?" His face was disturbingly close, forcing her to look directly into his eyes.

"I—I haven't changed. . . ."

His smile grew from a sunrise to a sunburst. "Oh, Kerry . . . sweet . . . my little love . . ." He gathered her firmly into his arms as he began to kiss away her tears.

She nestled closer against the roughness of his suit coat, not comprehending what was happening and afraid to question it for fear it might slip away. It was enough to hear his voice again, to allow his strength and closeness to bathe her in a joy she had thought forever lost.

He looked deeply into her eyes, and she felt him tremble slightly against her. "But why, when I tried to tell you how I felt—why did you run away from me?"

She couldn't think. "What do you mean?"

"In the kitchen, when I tried to make you listen to me."

Amazement replaced bewilderment. "You mean—you were trying to tell me . . . how you felt about me? I thought you were going to tell me about my da, and I couldn't

179

stand to face that shame with you watching—"

"Oh, Kerry," he moaned softly, shaking his head with dismay. "I thought you were repelled by me. Oh, my dear, there's so much I have to tell you—"

His eyes brimmed with wonder and tenderness, and a look of relief. "You really left because you love me? Because you thought I didn't—couldn't love you in return?"

When she nodded, he continued. "You felt that . . . you weren't good enough just because you're different from Emily?"

"Yes," she replied in a choked voice, wondering why he seemed to find the thought so difficult to comprehend. "I had begun to hope, just a little, after—after the way we kissed, that perhaps you did care for me. But when I found out about Da, I realized that I could simply never be the kind of lady you'd be wanting."

"Oh, my darling, darling girl." He stopped her words with a gentle touch of his fingers on her lips. "And I thought you could see my heart in my eyes every time I looked at you. . . ."

Kerry looked at him closely then—*really* looked at him, studying his gentle gaze. "What are you saying to me?"

She could see his pulse beating rapidly at the base of his throat. Her own heart was thumping loudly in her ears when he reached for her hands, grasping them firmly as he spoke. "I'm saying I love you, Kerry. I believe I've loved you since that first day when I saw you step off the steamer. I've loved you since I saw those copper curls of yours spilling out from the hood of your cape and your shamrock eyes challenging my claim that I was your guardian."

Kerry heard the tremor in his voice, saw the tender smile in his eyes, and wished she could simply stop time and make this moment last forever.

He tucked a curl, damp now from her tears, snugly behind her ear, then brushed a gentle kiss across her forehead. "I've denied my feelings a thousand times and more, believing if I didn't face them I'd be able to put them away because of your age—and mine. But the more I tried to ignore what I was feeling, the stronger the feelings became. Oh, Kerry, I do love you—in a way I have never loved another person, and never will."

"But—Emily?"

His smile was sad. "Emily was everything Molly told you she was—a sweet, dear woman." He paused for a long moment. "She was like a beloved sister to me. I did love her, Kerry, in a way that was special; and we were engaged. Both of our families assumed for years that we'd marry. We grew up together, you see—we were almost like family. I'm sure we would eventually have married, and probably would have even been happy." He settled her comfortably against his shoulder, combing her hair with gentle fingers as he went on to explain.

"I knew, though, that I really didn't feel about her as I should have, as a man needs to feel about the woman he's going to marry. For a long time after the accident, I felt so horribly guilty that I hadn't been able to care for her as she seemed to care for me."

She felt him draw in a long ragged breath. "So you see, dear, even though she was indeed a fine lady, that wasn't enough for me to love her . . . as I love you."

Kerry tipped her head to look up at him. "Truly, Jess? You truly do love me? As a woman, not as a younger sister?"

"More than life," he breathed fervently. "But, wait," he interrupted when she began to speak. "There's more you must know about your father."

"Oh, Jess," she protested quickly. "I don't think I want to know any more than I already do . . . ."

"No, no, dear—you don't understand. Everything wasn't in that letter. You see, your da didn't steal that money, but he was about to take the blame for the man who did."

"What?"

"That's right," he nodded, touching her cheek with the palm on one hand, smiling at her surprise. "The man who actually took those funds from the treasury had four small children and a wife who was ill. He stole the money out of sheer desperation, not knowing what else to do. His children were hungry, his wife was dying—Kerry, when your father learned about the situation he stepped in and insisted on bearing the blame. He knew that if the other man were to be arrested, he'd probably never get out of prison and his family would starve to death."

He framed her face between his hands and continued. "That's why Conor made all the arrangements for your guardianship so carefully—so he'd have the assurance that, no matter how long he might be imprisoned, you'd be cared for by someone he trusted . . . my father. But as it happened, your father died before there could even be a trial."

Slowly the cords of shame that had bound Kerry's heart for the past few hours began to break, freeing her to breathe deeply for what seemed to be the first time in an age.

"Is this all true, Jess?"

"It's all true, dear. So you see, your da was not only an honorable man—he was a noble man as well, a man who must have been especially pleasing to God."

"What do you mean?"

"Remember what our Lord said? *'Greater love hath no man than this, that a man lay down his life for his friend.'* He was talking about the kind of man your father was, Kerry—a very good man indeed, a man of great honor."

Grateful tears misted her eyes with a lovely shimmer. "So I still have the honor of my family, at least, to bring to you, Jess."

"Oh, Kerry," he murmured tenderly, "you don't have to bring anything to me except yourself, love." His arms

182

encircled her again, pulling her snugly against him. He spoke gently, but firmly. "I want to be very sure you understand this: I love you with all my heart, Kerry, because you're you. Not because of anything you've done or anything you have—but simply because you're Kerry . . . my sweet, adorable, wonderful Kerry."

He traced a light pattern across her brow and down her temple with one finger. "Promise me that you'll never forget this: When God looks at you—or at me, or at any one of His children—He doesn't see us with critical, measuring eyes. He doesn't look for imperfections or flaws or weaknesses. He doesn't see money or name or education or family. He looks at us from the cross . . . and He sees His own, His children, through eyes of love.

"And when I look at you, Kerry Shannon," he whispered, touching his lips to her cheek, "I can't see anything but love. . . ."

For several long, blissful moments they remained that way, Kerry wrapped snugly in his arms. Then, reluctantly, she broke the silence. "Jess? Don't be angry, but I must ask you one thing."

"What, dear?" he asked.

"What will you do about Edmund?"

He uttered a deep, exaggerated sigh, arched a knowing brow, and stared at her. "I have a choice, I suppose, of either bringing the wrath of the Irish down upon my head or bailing him out . . . again."

She nodded with relief, and smiled, flashing a dimple. Then she laid her cheek against his shoulder and exhaled a deep sigh of joy as she tried to absorb this miraculous thing that was happening. She felt his chin resting on the top of her head and, no longer able to contain her love for him, raised her face in search of his kiss, a kiss that was like a promise . . . a promise of everything good and wonderful and beautiful in life.

"I have something to ask you, love—but before you answer me, there's something you should know," he murmured into her hair.

"What, Jess?"

"There's a chance I may be leaving the Academy."

She held her breath. "But—why?"

"You asked me once why I stayed at West Point, remember?" When she nodded, he went on. "I've been doing a great deal of soul-searching lately, and I've begun to consider making a change. I've had strong feelings over the past few weeks that the Lord is trying to show me something, that He may be about to lead me in a different direction. More and more, I feel the need to serve where I might be able to have more influence politically, where I could perhaps deal more directly with the slavery issue, with the problems of immigrants and factory workers, and—well, you know the things that grieve my heart. Kerry, there's a possibility of my going to Washington. I'm not certain just yet—but I am thinking about it."

Squeezing her hands tightly in his, he said urgently, "Kerry, love, I'm not sure yet what I may do. I still have responsibilities at West Point. Might be a year—or even more—before I make a move. But I sense a change is coming. And I thought you should know about all this before I ask you . . . if you'll be my wife."

"Oh, Jess! Are you sure? I mean, a man such as you—so famous and fine and—" His warning frown made her falter. She swallowed hard before making one last plea for reassurance. "You're certain? Even if you go to Washington?"

He smiled down at her, his eyes misting with love, as he declared, in a brogue that would have done Molly proud, "A famous man such as I, Kerry Shannon, must be havin' a fine lady at his side, especially if he's on his way to Washington."

His arms closed snugly around her, and he gently

184

brushed a straying curl away from her cheek with his lips before whispering, "Will you be my lady then, Kerry Shannon? Will you be my wife . . . my love?"

She smiled against his bearded cheek, then pulled back just enough to search for something in his eyes. Finding it, she announced in her delightfully throaty voice, "I will always be your lady, my Jess. Always."

EPILOGUE

Kerry lowered her flute from her lips and peeked out her upstairs window, hiding herself behind the corner of the draperies so that Jess, who was pacing the yard below, couldn't see her standing there in her camisole and petticoats. She smiled mischievously as she watched him walk back and forth across the snow-covered path. His hands were bunched in tight fists behind his back, and he continually clenched and unclenched them in an anxious gesture. Periodically he would brush imaginary specks from the shoulders of his severe black swallowtail coat, then automatically make a smoothing motion on his stiff white collar.

The bright green eyes watching him sparkled with a mixture of love and amusement. *Whatever is he doing out there in the cold? Is he so nervous he's forgotten it's midwinter?* Even if Molly hadn't given her a detailed description of the prospective groom's early-morning anxiety,

Kerry would have been able to see it in his mannerisms.

When he suddenly turned and looked up toward her window, she retreated even further behind the draperies, giggling. Would he be embarrassed to know how dear and funny he appeared to her this morning?

"Faith, and I don't believe what I'm seeing!" the scandalized voice of Molly came bursting through the bedroom door. "An hour away from the wedding and here you stand in your petticoats playing your flute. Are you daft, Kerry O'Neill?"

Kerry made a vain attempt to stifle a merry ripple of laughter, her failure to do so agitating the housekeeper even more. Molly grabbed the flute and placed it firmly on the window seat, then crossed her arms impatiently. With one of her fiercest glares, she began a colorful tirade of what was going to happen if a certain young bride-to-be did not immediately cease her foolishness and don her wedding gown.

"But, Molly, just look at him. Watch how he paces."

Stealing a quick glance out of the window, Molly denied herself the smile that teased at the corners of her mouth. "Aye, and you're a fine pair, you are. Both of you with minds gone to mush this day. I'll be fair to drop when all this fuss is over. Now get away from that window, lass, and into your gown—at once."

"Oh, I have time, Molly. Don't be angry with me now. Sure, and I won't be late for my own wedding."

"Well, I should hope not!" Molly snorted. "Not after all the fret and fuss it's taken to get us to this day." With a meaningful look, she turned to gather the wedding dress from the bed.

"You're a grand-looking sight yourself this morning," Kerry complimented sincerely. "Like a queen, I'm thinking."

"Oh, get on with you! It's into that dress now, Miss, so we can get your hair up."

"No." Kerry's voice was firm. "Jess does not like my hair up. I'll be wearing it down just as I always do." She gave a defiant toss of her head.

"Ach! *Jess does not like my hair up,* '" Molly mimicked. "Tuck it under a kerchief then, for all I'm caring. Hold still now and let me get these buttons. Sam Grant will be here any minute to take Jess away to the chapel. If you'll not have me tellin' the both of them you've lost your wits and cannot be wed this day, you'd best be doing as you're told."

Jess was absolutely convinced his heart was about to stop as he watched Kerry proceed down the aisle on the arm of Edmund Teague. He was dimly aware of little else other than the vision in ivory silk and lace approaching him from the rear of the chapel. The majesty of the organ faded as the roar of his own heartbeat swelled. Sam Grant, standing quietly beside him, gave his arm a brief, reassuring touch. A fog of smiling cadet faces drifted in and out of his consciousness, and he irrationally wondered if any man had ever become speechless at the altar. Certainly, he was about to.

I shall choke if I open my mouth . . . . I have no breath . . . I can't even swallow . . . Oh, Father, isn't she lovely? Isn't she exquisite? And to think she doesn't consider herself a lady . . . . Well, she's finer and more precious than any other lady in the world, in my eyes. Thank You for allowing me to love her, for letting her be mine . . . . With all my heart and all my soul, Lord, I promise to love and to honor her . . . Oh, my dear Lord, thank You!

Kerry was certain she would stumble before reaching the end of the long—ever so long—aisle, though Edmund, bless him, had a firm grip on her arm.

Oh, Father, would You just be helping me to get down

189

*there to Jess without tripping and embarrassing him? He's
gone to so much trouble and expense for all this, You see.
Poor man, getting himself a bride with no dowry . . . a bride
who could not even buy her own gown. But my Jess said
that was a silly thing to fret about.*

*Ah, just look at him, Father. Isn't he grand? He looks proud,
I'm thinking, and a bit frightened as well. Oh, my—that must
be his friend who's to marry us, the Reverend Mr. Henry Ward
Beecher, standing there. Why, he has a twinkle in his eye, I do
believe. Yes, he would appear to be a kind man, like my Jess.
Molly looks so proud, sitting there . . . oh, she's—can it be—
why, Molly's crying! Just as my own mother would no doubt
be crying, could she be with me on this day . . . .*

*However can I thank You for all this, Lord? Sure, and
You've blessed me far beyond what I've any right to dream
of . . . but I promise You this—and we O'Neills always keep
our promises, as You know—I promise to love and to honor
this man, Lord, for as long as I live . . . aye, for a lifetime
and more. . . .*

Jess took her arm. She could feel him trembling even as
he gave her hand a quick squeeze beneath her lovely bou-
quet. She looked up at him, her eyes almost hidden behind
the mist of veil. His face was flushed, and there was a thin
line of perspiration across his forehead. But when his gaze
melted into hers, he began to smile the dearest, most tender smile she'd ever seen upon his face.

*"Dearly beloved, we are gathered together here in the
sight of God and in the presence of these witnesses, to join
this man and this woman . . ."*

Both of them started with surprise when the entire cadet
congregation, in answer to the minister's question, *"Who
giveth this woman to be married to this man?"* stood, and in
unison, replied, "We do!"

". . . I, Jess Andrew Dalton, take thee, Kerry Shannon
O'Neill, to be my beloved wife, to have and to hold, from

this day forward. I vow to love thee, to cherish thee, in sickness and in health, in riches or in poverty, and to honor thee and care for thee so long as I live . . . I pledge to thee my worldly possessions, my respect, and my fidelity for now and forever."

". . . I, Kerry Shannon O'Neill, take thee, Jess Andrew Dalton, to be my beloved husband, to have and to hold, from this day forward. I vow to love thee, to honor and cling to thee in sickness and in health, in riches or in poverty . . . and I pledge to thee my worldly possessions, my respect, and my fidelity for now and forever."

". . . *May God the Father, Son, and Spirit look upon each of you and your union with favor, blessing, and love . . . May you live together in this life with love and loyalty, joined with our God and Lord for all eternity . . . . Amen.*"

Jess raised her veil at a nudge from Sam, gave her a long, steady look that held many promises, and with lips that trembled until the instant they met hers, kissed her, whispering, "Forever, my love . . . ."

They walked the aisle together this time, stopping to hug and kiss Molly. Then, passing row after row of beaming cadets standing at attention, they quickened their pace.

Winter sunshine greeted their radiant faces when the chapel doors were flung open. Clinging to each other and their shining new happiness, they left the chapel beneath a canopy of crossed swords and a bright blue heaven.

Waving one last time to the crowd of cheering well-wishers, the new Mrs. Dalton allowed her husband to assist her into an elegant carriage driven by a smiling Sam Grant. The groom, seated as closely as possible to his bride, treated himself to an unhurried kiss, then leaned forward to give their uniformed driver his instructions.

A fleeting picture brought a mysterious smile to Kerry O'Neill Dalton's glowing face as the carriage began to move away from the chapel: a glimpse, quickly gone, of a proud and smiling Irishman, who winked and waved his cap in the air in a happy salute to the day.

Book Two of *The Dalton Saga, A Whisper in the Wind,* continues the story of Kerry and Jess. Confronted with hatred, terror, and tragedy, the couple struggles to hold on to their love and faith.